Practical Data Modeling

A Step-by-Step Guide Across Industries

Michael E. Kirshteyn, Ph.D

Disclaimer

This book is intended for educational purposes only. The information contained within is provided to help readers gain a general understanding of logical data modeling principles and techniques. While every effort has been made to ensure accuracy, the author and publisher make no warranties, express or implied, regarding the content's correctness, completeness, or suitability for any specific purpose.

The examples, exercises, and case studies included are illustrative and simplified for instructional purposes. They may not reflect the full complexity or specific legal, regulatory, or technical requirements of particular industries or individual projects. Readers should exercise independent judgment and consult with relevant professionals, such as data architects, database administrators, legal experts, or compliance officers, when applying these concepts in real-world contexts.

The author and publisher assume no responsibility for any damages or losses resulting from the use of this book. The reader assumes full responsibility for the application of information presented herein and acknowledges that the field of data modeling is evolving, with standards, practices, and tools subject to change.

All trademarks, logos, and industry references included in this book are the property of their respective owners and are used here solely for illustrative and educational purposes.

Acknowledgements

Creating this book has been a collaborative effort, and I am deeply grateful to everyone who supported me in bringing it to life.

First and foremost, I want to thank my family and friends for their unwavering encouragement and patience throughout the writing process. Their belief in me has been a constant source of inspiration.

I am also grateful to the talented professionals in the field of data modeling, data architecture, and database administration whose insights have helped shape the material presented here. The knowledge and experiences shared by colleagues and mentors have greatly enriched my understanding of logical data modeling.

A special thank you to my editor, who provided invaluable feedback and guidance. Their meticulous attention to detail and commitment to clarity have improved this work immensely.

To the technical reviewers, your expertise and keen insights have ensured that the content is both accurate and practical. I deeply appreciate the time and care you took to review the material and provide constructive feedback.

A special acknowledgment is extended to the ChatGPT team for their groundbreaking language model. ChatGPT's contributions have been instrumental in refining the language and ensuring clarity in conveying complex concepts within this comprehensive guide. Your innovative technology has truly enriched the content and elevated its overall quality.

Deepest appreciation to the Night Café team for gracing our front cover with their mesmerizing and exquisite artwork. Their visionary talent has elevated this publication, captivating readers from the very first glance

Finally, I would like to extend my gratitude to the readers. Your curiosity, dedication, and passion for learning are the true driving forces behind this book. It is my hope that this resource serves you well on your journey to mastering logical data modeling.

Thank you all for your contributions to this project. This book would not have been possible without your support.

Abstract

"Practical Data Modeling: A Step-by-Step Guide Across Industries" is a comprehensive guide designed to provide IT professionals, data architects, and aspiring data modelers with practical, hands-on exercises to deepen their understanding of logical data modeling concepts. This workbook builds on the foundation laid in my first book, *Mastering Data Modeling: From Concepts to Practical Implementation*, expanding on its principles with a focus on industry-specific applications and real-world scenarios.

Through detailed case studies, industry-specific examples, and a series of structured exercises, this workbook walks readers through the process of constructing conceptual and logical models for various sectors, including healthcare, finance, retail, telecommunications, and more. Key topics covered include entity identification, relationship modeling, cardinality, and advanced techniques such as normalization and data integrity.

Designed for both beginner and intermediate IT professionals, this workbook emphasizes practical skills and provides the tools necessary to create effective, accurate, and scalable data models. With the addition of exercises at the end of each chapter, readers will gain experience in applying the concepts to real-world data challenges, honing their skills in logical data modeling.

Whether you're looking to enhance your knowledge after reading "Mastering Data Modeling" or you're starting your journey in data modeling, this workbook is an essential resource to guide you through the complexities of logical modeling with clarity and precision.

***

Table of Contents

***

Introduction

Purpose of the Workbook

Welcome to the *Practical Data Modeling: A Step-by-Step Guide Across Industries*, designed to guide IT professionals, especially beginners, through the essential principles of logical data modeling. Whether you're an aspiring data architect, database designer, or system analyst, this workbook will provide the practical knowledge you need to build robust data models that support your organization's data needs. The goal of this workbook is to offer a hands-on approach to learning logical data modeling, with real-world exercises and case studies that help you understand how to apply theoretical concepts in a practical environment. This workbook is also designed to integrate 7 Data Decomposition Constructs throughout its chapters to help you structure data in a more granular and functional way.

Who This Book is For

This workbook is intended for IT professionals who are new to logical data modeling but have a basic understanding of data structures and relational databases. Whether you're learning to design a database, improve an existing one, or transition to a role that involves data architecture, this book will help you acquire the skills needed to model data logically and efficiently. Additionally, if you're involved in data-driven decision-making or building data-centric applications, this book will help you understand how to structure data effectively for long-term success.

Learning Objectives

By the end of this workbook, you will be able to:

- Identify and define key data modeling concepts such as entities, attributes, and relationships.

- Create logical data models that reflect real-world business processes.

- Understand how to use the 7 Data Decomposition Constructs (Parties, Products and Services, Location, Transaction/Event, Processes, Rules and Regulations, and Resources) to better structure your models.

- Use industry-specific examples and case studies to understand how logical data models are applied across different sectors.

- Gain proficiency in using both Lucidchart and ERwin, two powerful tools for diagramming and creating data models.

Overview of Logical Data Modeling Concepts

Logical data modeling is the process of defining the structure of data without considering how it will be physically implemented in a database. It involves identifying the key entities (such as customers, products, or transactions), their attributes (the properties or characteristics of those entities), and the relationships between these entities. Logical data models serve as blueprints for building databases and help ensure that the system will support business requirements and data integrity.

Michael E. Kirshteyn, Ph.D

Key concepts in logical data modeling include:

- **Entities**: These represent objects or concepts in the business, such as a person, order, or product.

- **Attributes**: The properties or characteristics of entities. For example, a customer entity may have attributes such as name, address, and contact information.

- **Relationships**: These describe how entities are connected to each other. A customer might place an order, for example, forming a relationship between the customer and the order.

- **Cardinality**: The number of occurrences of one entity related to occurrences of another entity, such as one-to-many or many-to-many.

- **Primary Keys**: Unique identifiers for entities that ensure data integrity and enable efficient data retrieval.

Throughout the workbook, we will also incorporate the 7 Data Decomposition Constructs into each model, helping you break down the data into actionable components:

1. **Parties:** Identifying the entities that interact with your system (e.g., Customers, Suppliers).

2. **Products and Services:** The core offerings of the business (e.g., Products, Orders).

3. **Location:** Geographical or physical aspects (e.g., Store Locations, Customer Addresses).

4. **Transaction/Event:** The events or actions that drive business operations (e.g., Purchase Orders, Payments).

5. **Processes:** The workflows and business processes that govern data (e.g., Order Fulfillment).

6. **Rules and Regulations:** Legal, compliance, or business rules that affect data (e.g., Sales Tax Calculations, Product Returns).

7. **Resources:** Assets that are necessary for business functions (e.g., Inventory, Employees).

How to Use This Workbook

The *Practical Data Modeling: A Step-by-Step Guide Across Industries* is designed to be both a practical guide and a learning resource. Each chapter includes clear explanations, hands-on exercises, and real-world case studies that allow you to practice the concepts you're learning.

To get the most out of this workbook, follow these steps:

1. **Read the Concepts**: Start by reading the theoretical explanation of each concept in the chapter.

2. **Work through the Exercises**: After understanding the key concepts, complete the exercises to reinforce your learning and gain practical experience.

3. **Review the Case Studies**: The case studies at the end of each chapter provide examples of data modeling in real-world scenarios. Use them to see how the concepts are applied in practice.

4. **Take the Quiz**: Each chapter ends with a quiz that helps you test your understanding of the material.

Michael E. Kirshteyn, Ph.D

By completing each chapter, you will gradually build your expertise in logical data modeling, developing a clear understanding of how to create data models that reflect business needs and data integrity standards.

Key Tools: Lucidchart and ERwin Approach

This workbook emphasizes two powerful tools for data modeling: Lucidchart and ERwin. While Lucidchart is an intuitive, cloud-based diagramming tool, ERwin is a more advanced, industry-standard data modeling tool that is widely used for enterprise-level data modeling.

Throughout the workbook, the exercises and examples will use Lucidchart for diagramming the data models, but the instructions will describe the steps as if using ERwin, which is commonly used by data professionals in the industry. This will allow you to practice data modeling using both tools, ensuring that you're prepared to use whichever tool is best suited for your organization's needs.

Both Lucidchart and ERwin are capable of generating entity-relationship diagrams (ERDs), setting primary keys, and specifying cardinality, all of which are central to logical data modeling. You will learn to use these tools effectively as you create and refine your data models in the exercises.

By the end of this workbook, you will be proficient in logical data modeling concepts, and you will be able to apply these concepts to create accurate, efficient data models for a variety of industries.

Michael E. Kirshteyn, Ph.D

Michael E. Kirshteyn, Ph.D

Chapter 1: Foundations of Logical Data Modeling

Introduction to Logical Data Modeling

Logical data modeling is an essential part of designing efficient and effective databases that support business operations and decision-making. It serves as the blueprint for structuring data, ensuring that all relevant entities, their attributes, and the relationships between them are properly defined. Logical data modeling abstracts away the physical aspects of how data is stored in a database, focusing instead on the logical organization and flow of information.

In this chapter, we will introduce you to the fundamental principles of logical data modeling. You will learn the basic components of a data model and how they interact with each other. This chapter provides the foundational knowledge you need to build a logical data model that accurately represents the data structures required for any business domain.

Key Concepts: Entities, Attributes, Relationships, Cardinality, and Primary and Foreign Keys

To create an effective logical data model, you need to understand the key concepts that form its core: entities, attributes, relationships, cardinality, and primary keys. Let's explore each of these in detail:

1. Entities

Entities represent real-world objects or concepts within a business domain. An entity can be something tangible, like a Product or Customer, or abstract, like a Transaction or Event. In a data model, entities are typically represented as tables or objects. Each entity is defined by its attributes and the relationships it shares with other entities.

Examples:

- **Customer**: Represents a person or organization that purchases goods or services.

- **Product**: Represents an item available for sale.

- **Order**: Represents a transaction in which a customer purchases one or more products.

Entities in Subject Area - Sales

- Customer

- Attributes: CustomerID (PK), Name, Email, Phone, Address

- Relationships: Places Orders (1:M relationship with Order)

- Order

- Attributes: OrderID (PK), OrderDate, TotalAmount, CustomerID (FK)

- Relationships: Contains Products (M:M relationship with Product)

- Product

- Attributes: ProductID (PK), Description, Price, StockQuantity

- Relationships: Appears in Orders (M:M relationship with Order)

- Payment

- Attributes: PaymentID (PK), PaymentDate, Amount, OrderID (FK)

- Relationships: Linked to Orders (1:1 relationship with Order)

2. Attributes

Attributes are the properties or characteristics of an entity. They describe the specific details associated with each entity. For example, a Customer entity might have attributes like Name, Address, and Email Address. These attributes are usually mapped to columns in a database table.

Examples:

- Customer: *Name, Email, Phone Number*

- Product: *Product ID, Description, Price*

3. Relationships

Relationships define how entities are connected to each other. These connections reflect how real-world processes interact with the data. A relationship between two entities can be one-to-one, one-to-many, or many-to-many, depending on how the entities interact.

Example:

- A **Customer** places an **Order** – this defines a relationship between the Customer and Order entities.

Michael E. Kirshteyn, Ph.D

Relationships in Subject Area - Sales

- Customer to Order: One-to-many (1:M), a customer can place multiple orders, but each order is placed by only one customer.

- Order to Product: Many-to-many (M:M), an order can contain multiple products, and a product can appear in multiple orders.

- Order to Payment: One-to-one (1:1), each order is linked to one payment.

4. Cardinality

ERD Cardinalty

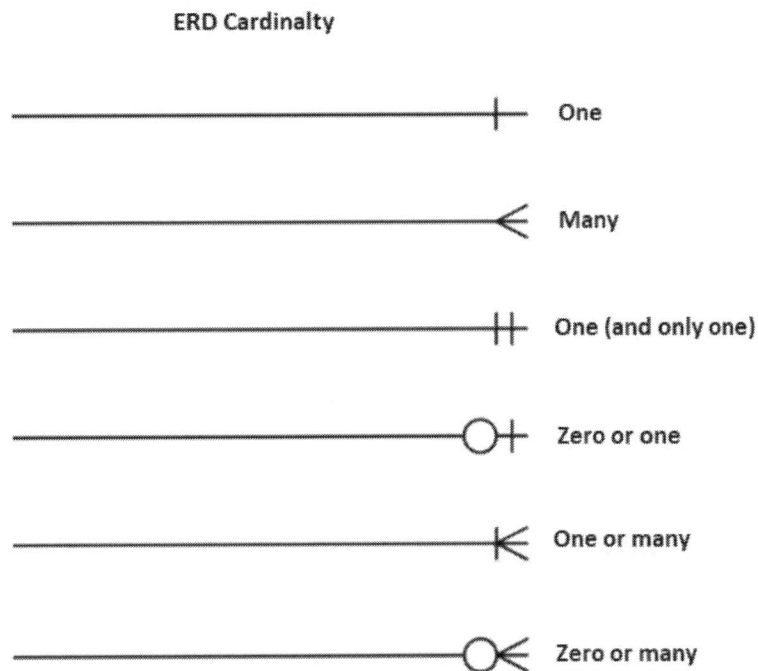

Cardinality refers to the number of instances of one entity that are related to instances of another entity. It is crucial in defining the relationship between entities. Cardinality helps in understanding the data flow and how records in different entities should be linked.

Types of Cardinality:

- One-to-One (1:1): Each instance of an entity is related to exactly one instance of another entity.

- Example: A **Customer** has one Loyalty Card.

- **One-to-Many (1:M):** An instance of one entity can be related to multiple instances of another entity, but each instance of the second entity is related to only one instance of the first.

  - Example: A **Customer** can place multiple **Orders,** but each **Order** is placed by only one **Customer.**

- **Many-to-Many (M:M):** Instances of both entities can be related to multiple instances of the other.

  - Example: **Students** can enroll in many **Courses**, and each **Course** can have many **Students**.

5. Primary Keys

A Primary Key is a field (or a combination of fields) in a database table that uniquely identifies each record in that table. It ensures that each entry in the table is distinct and can be reliably accessed or referenced. A primary key must meet the following conditions:

- **Uniqueness:** Each value in the primary key column(s) must be unique.

- **Non-nullability:** The primary key cannot contain null values, ensuring that every record has a valid identifier.

- **Immutability:** Ideally, a primary key's value should not change once it is set, ensuring data consistency.

For example, in a Customer table, the CustomerID field might be used as the primary key, uniquely identifying each customer in the database.

Examples:

- **Customer:** *CustomerID* (Primary Key)

- **Product:** *ProductID* (Primary Key)

6. Foreign Keys

A Foreign Key is a field (or a combination of fields) in a database table that establishes a link between data in two tables. It references the Primary Key of another table, creating a relationship between the two tables. The purpose of the foreign key is to maintain referential integrity by ensuring that every foreign key value in one table corresponds to an existing primary key value in another table.

Unlike a primary key, a foreign key does not have to be unique and can accept null values, meaning that it's possible for some records to not be linked to another table.

For example, in an **Order** table, the **CustomerID** field might be used as a foreign key that links each order to a specific customer in the **Customer** table. This ensures that every order is associated with a valid customer, enforcing data consistency.

Identifying and Non-Identifying Relationships

In data modeling, understanding relationships between entities is crucial. Relationships can be classified as *identifying* or *non-identifying*, and each type plays a specific role in data integrity and model design.

- **Identifying Relationships**: An identifying relationship occurs when a child entity cannot exist without a parent entity. In this case, the child entity's primary key includes the parent's primary key as a component, making the relationship fundamental to the entity's identity.

  - *Example*: In an "Order Item" table linked to an "Order" table, each order item exists only as part of an order, creating an identifying relationship.

- **Non-Identifying Relationships**: A non-identifying relationship exists when the child entity can exist independently of the parent entity. Here, the foreign key relationship does not affect the child's primary key; the parent's primary key appears as a foreign key in the child entity.

  - *Example*: A "Customer" and "Order" table might be connected by a non-identifying relationship, where an order is associated with a customer, but each order is uniquely identifiable without including the customer's primary key.

Understanding these distinctions aids in establishing clear rules for data dependency and integrity across entities in a logical model.

Understanding Relationship Lines in Logical Models

In logical data models, the type of line connecting entities—whether solid or dotted—holds significance, as it visually conveys the nature of the relationship between entities. This differentiation helps modelers understand how entities depend on or relate to each other structurally and in terms of data integrity. Here's a breakdown:

1. **Solid Lines**: Solid lines represent *identifying relationships*. In an identifying relationship, the child entity's existence is tied to the parent entity. This means that the child entity's primary key is partially or fully dependent on the parent entity's primary key, making it uniquely identifiable

only in the context of that parent entity. For example, an OrderLine entity cannot exist without an associated Order, as the unique identity of OrderLine entries is dependent on the Order entity.

2. **Dotted or Dashed Lines**: Dotted or dashed lines indicate *non-identifying relationships*, where the child entity can exist independently of the parent entity. In these relationships, the parent entity's primary key does not form part of the child entity's primary key. For instance, an Order can exist separately from a Customer, so the Order and Customer relationship is non-identifying.

3. **Optional and Dependency Relationships**: Dotted lines can also depict optional or weakly dependent relationships. For example, in a Manager and Employee relationship, not all employees may have a manager, so the relationship may be represented with a dotted line to indicate its optionality.

These conventions aid in distinguishing relationships and defining how entities connect in terms of dependency, optionality, and integrity constraints.

Data Modeling Notations: Choosing the Right Visual Representation

In data modeling, various notations can be used to represent entities, relationships, and cardinality in a logical model. Each notation has its strengths, and the choice of notation can affect how easily a model is interpreted by others. This subsection will review the most common notations, their pros and cons, and recommended usage scenarios. In this workbook, we will use **Crow's Foot notation** due to its clarity and widespread use in the industry.

1. Crow's Foot Notation

  - **Description**: Uses symbols resembling a crow's foot to indicate "many" in relationships. Lines and symbols denote one-to-one, one-to-many, and many-to-many relationships.

  - **Pros**: Clear visual cues; widely understood and supported in most modeling tools.

  - **Cons**: Limited to representing cardinality, lacks detail for complex business rules.

  - **Recommended Use**: Best for straightforward models where clarity and ease of understanding are priorities. Ideal for beginners and standard business applications.

2. Chen Notation

  - **Description**: Uses ovals to represent attributes, and relationships are shown as diamonds connecting rectangular entities.

  - **Pros**: Good for representing attributes explicitly and emphasizing entity-relationship structures.

- **Cons**: Can be cumbersome for large models, as the details can lead to clutter.

- **Recommended Use**: Suitable for small-scale models and academic settings where focus on entity-relationship theory is desired.

3. **UML (Unified Modeling Language) Notation**

- **Description**: Part of the UML standard, this notation represents entities as classes with attributes, while relationships are depicted with connectors.

- **Pros**: Versatile, supports complex scenarios including inheritance and polymorphism, suitable for object-oriented databases.

- **Cons**: Requires a deeper understanding of UML; less intuitive for relational data modeling.

- **Recommended Use**: Well-suited for complex applications, especially in software engineering contexts where object-oriented principles are in use.

4. **IDEF1X Notation**

- **Description**: Uses boxes and lines to represent entities and relationships with arrows to indicate relationships.

- **Pros**: Offers a high level of detail and precision, suitable for large enterprise models.

- **Cons**: Complex to learn and not as widely recognized outside of specialized fields.

- **Recommended Use**: Ideal for detailed, enterprise-scale models where precision is required.

In this workbook, we'll use **Crow's Foot notation** due to its simplicity and effectiveness in representing the core concepts of logical data modeling. Crow's Foot notation will help you focus on the relationships and cardinality between entities without getting lost in visual complexity.

Understanding Subject Areas in Data Models

In logical data modeling, large datasets are often divided into smaller, more manageable sections known as subject areas. Each subject area corresponds to a specific business domain or function, such as sales, inventory, or customer management.

When creating a data model, subject areas help to organize the data into logical groupings based on the business requirements. By breaking the data model into subject areas, you can maintain a clearer structure, improve performance, and ensure that relationships are well-defined.

Michael E. Kirshteyn, Ph.D

Examples of Subject Areas:

- **Sales:** Customer orders, sales transactions, and product sales.

- **Inventory:** Stock levels, product information, and supplier details.

- **Customer** Management: Customer profiles, contact details, and service records.

The Role of Conceptual, Logical, and Physical Data Models

In the world of data modeling, it's essential to distinguish between three different types of models: conceptual, logical, and physical.

1. Conceptual Data Model:

This model provides a high-level overview of the system, focusing on identifying key entities and their relationships without getting into implementation details. It's a simple representation of the business domain and is often used in the early stages of design.

2. Logical Data Model:

The logical data model builds on the conceptual model by adding more detail and defining the attributes, relationships, and cardinality of the entities. It does not consider physical storage or database-specific details. This is the model you'll focus on in this workbook.

3. Physical Data Model:

The physical data model takes the logical model and refines it for implementation. It focuses on how the data will be stored, indexed, and optimized in a specific database management system (DBMS). It includes details like table structures, data types, and storage considerations.

Common Pitfalls and Best Practices for Beginners

When starting out with logical data modeling, there are several common mistakes that beginners often make. Here are some tips to avoid these pitfalls:

Michael E. Kirshteyn, Ph.D

- Overcomplicating the model: Beginners often try to include every possible detail in the model, making it overly complex. Keep it simple and focused on business needs.

- Ignoring business rules: It's important to work closely with business stakeholders to ensure that the model reflects actual business requirements.

- Failing to define relationships: Properly defining relationships between entities ensures data integrity and avoids data redundancy.

- Inconsistent naming conventions: Always use consistent naming conventions for entities, attributes, and relationships to make the model easier to understand.

Best Practices:

- Start with a high-level conceptual model, then gradually add detail to create the logical model.

- Use clear, descriptive names for entities and attributes to avoid confusion.

- Document assumptions and business rules that influence the model.

- Regularly validate the model with business stakeholders to ensure it aligns with real-world data needs.

Hands-On Exercise: Building a Simple Data Model

In this exercise, you will create a simple data model for an online store. This will involve identifying key entities, their attributes, and relationships. Follow the steps below:

1. Identify the main entities: What are the primary objects in the business? For an online store, entities might include *Customer*, *Product*, *Order*, and *Payment*.

2. Define the attributes: What properties are associated with each entity? For Customer, you might have attributes like *CustomerID*, *Name*, and *Email*.

3. Establish relationships: How are the entities related? For example, a *Customer* places an *Order*.

4. Define cardinality: What type of relationship is it? A *Customer* can place multiple *Orders*, but each *Order* is linked to only one *Customer*.

Use Lucidchart or ERwin to diagram your model and ensure that you correctly define relationships and cardinality.

Chapter Summary and Quiz

In this chapter, we introduced you to the fundamentals of logical data modeling, including key concepts like entities, attributes, relationships, cardinality, and primary keys. We discussed how subject areas help organize large data models and the distinctions between conceptual, logical, and physical data models. Lastly, we covered common pitfalls and best practices to keep in mind as you begin your journey into data modeling.

Quiz:

1. What is the primary difference between a conceptual, logical, and physical data model?

2.

 Define cardinality and explain the three main types of cardinality.

3. What are the key components of a data model?

4. What is the purpose of defining primary keys in a data model?

5. In the online store example, what entities and relationships did you identify?

This concludes Chapter 1! Be sure to review the concepts, complete the exercises, and test your understanding with the quiz. Next, we'll move into industry-specific examples, where we'll build on these foundations.

Chapter 2: Data Modeling for the Retail Industry

Industry Overview: Structure, Operations, and Key Data Elements

The retail industry is a dynamic and fast-paced sector that involves the sale of goods and services to consumers. Retail businesses can range from small, independent stores to large multinational chains, both operating through physical stores, e-commerce platforms, or a combination of both. The key to success in retail is a deep understanding of consumer behavior, inventory management, sales performance, and customer engagement.

Retail operations typically involve the following key functions:

- **Sales**: The process of selling products to customers, including point-of-sale (POS) transactions, online sales, and promotions.

- **Inventory**: The management of stock levels, suppliers, and product availability.

- **Customer Management**: The processes related to tracking customer behavior, purchases, preferences, and loyalty programs.

- **Supply Chain Management**: The movement of goods from suppliers to stores or warehouses.

The key data elements in retail include:

- **Products**: Descriptions, pricing, inventory levels, and suppliers.

- **Customers**: Personal information, purchase history, preferences, and loyalty status.

- **Transactions**: Purchase details, quantities, pricing, discounts, and payment methods.

- **Stores**: Location data, store performance, and staffing.

- **Suppliers**: Information related to the sourcing and replenishment of products.

Identifying High-Level Entities in Retail

To construct an effective retail data model, it is essential to identify the primary entities that will capture all aspects of the retail operation. At a high level, the following entities are critical in the retail industry:

1. **Product**: Products are the items being sold in the retail environment. A product entity captures the details necessary for pricing, categorization, and stock management.

2. **Customer**: The customer entity captures personal and transactional data about those who purchase goods or services.

3. **Order**: Orders capture the purchase of products by customers, often involving payment and shipment processes.

4. **Payment**: Payments are necessary for tracking financial transactions linked to orders.

5. **Supplier**: Suppliers ensure the availability of products by providing goods to retail businesses.

6. **Store**: In the case of physical retail, stores represent individual retail locations that manage sales, inventory, and customer interactions.

7. **Inventory**: This represents the availability of products at various stores or warehouses.

Essential Retail Components and Attributes

Retail data modeling requires an understanding of the key components that form the foundation of a retail data model. These components are typically represented by entities, and each entity has a set of attributes. Below are the essential components of a retail data model:

- **Product**: The central entity in retail, representing the goods or services available for sale.

  - Attributes: ProductID (PK), Description, Price, Category, SupplierID, StockQuantity, DiscountRate

- **Customer**: Represents individuals or organizations who make purchases.

  - Attributes: CustomerID (PK), Name, Address, Email, Phone, LoyaltyPoints

- **Order**: Represents a customer's purchase, whether online or in-store.

  - Attributes: OrderID (PK), OrderDate, CustomerID (FK), TotalAmount, PaymentStatus

- **Payment**: Represents the payment transactions associated with an order.

  - Attributes: PaymentID (PK), OrderID (FK), PaymentDate, Amount, PaymentMethod

- **Supplier**: Represents businesses or entities that provide products to the retailer.

  - Attributes: SupplierID (PK), Name, ContactInfo, LeadTime, ProductID (FK)

- **Store**: Represents physical locations where products are sold.

  - Attributes: StoreID (PK), StoreName, Location, ManagerID

- **Inventory**: Represents stock levels at each store or warehouse.

  - Attributes: ProductID (FK), StoreID (FK), QuantityAvailable, LastRestockDate

Constructing the Conceptual Model

The conceptual model serves as the first step in building a data model. It is a high-level, business-oriented model that identifies the entities, their attributes, and the relationships between them. At this stage, the focus is on understanding the core business operations, not on database-specific details.

In the retail industry, a conceptual model might look like this:

1. **Entities**: Product, Customer, Order, Payment, Supplier, Store, Inventory

2. **Relationships**:

   - A **Customer** places an **Order** (1:M relationship).

   - An **Order** contains multiple **Products** (M:M relationship).

   - A **Supplier** provides multiple **Products** (1:M relationship).

   - A **Product** is available in multiple **Stores** (M:M relationship).

   - An **Order** is paid by a **Payment** (1:1 relationship).

   - A **Store** has multiple **Inventory** records for various **Products** (1:M relationship).

The conceptual model allows business stakeholders to confirm the relationships and entities before diving into more detailed modeling.

Dividing the Model into Subject Areas: Sales, Inventory, Customer Management

To manage the complexity of a retail data model, it is helpful to divide the model into subject areas. Each subject area captures a specific area of the retail operation and is responsible for a subset of the data model.

1. **Sales**: This subject area captures all data related to customer transactions, including orders, payments, and product sales.

   - Key entities: Order, Payment, Product, Customer, Store

   - Example: A customer places an order that includes multiple products, with payments tied to each order.

2. **Inventory**: This subject area tracks the availability and movement of products in and out of stores or warehouses.

   - Key entities: Product, Inventory, Store, Supplier

   - Example: A store's inventory is updated each time products are restocked by suppliers or sold to customers.

3. **Customer Management**: This subject area manages customer profiles, purchase history, loyalty programs, and other customer-centric data.

   - Key entities: Customer, Order, Payment, LoyaltyPoints

   - Example: A customer's purchase history informs targeted promotions or loyalty rewards.

Cardinality and Relationships in Retail Data Models

When defining relationships in retail data models, it's essential to identify the correct cardinality to ensure data consistency and integrity. Below are some common relationships and their cardinalities in retail data models:

1. **Customer to Order**: One-to-many (1:M). A customer can place multiple orders, but each order is linked to only one customer.

2. **Order to Product**: Many-to-many (M:M). An order can contain multiple products, and a product can appear in multiple orders.

3. **Product to Supplier**: One-to-many (1:M). A supplier can provide multiple products, but each product is sourced from a single supplier.

4. **Order to Payment**: One-to-one (1:1). Each order corresponds to a single payment transaction.

Michael E. Kirshteyn, Ph.D

5. **Store to Inventory**: One-to-many (1:M). Each store manages multiple inventory records for various products.

Many-to-Many Relationships Through Associative (Bridge) Tables

In some cases, a relationship between two entities is more complex than a simple one-to-one or one-to-many relationship. When each instance of an entity can relate to multiple instances of another entity, and vice versa, we encounter a **many-to-many** (M:M) relationship. However, relational databases do not directly support many-to-many relationships, so they need to be broken down into simpler relationships using an **associative (bridge) table**.

What is a Bridge Table?

A **bridge table**, also known as an **associative table**, is an intermediary table that resolves many-to-many relationships. It contains foreign keys pointing to the primary keys of the two entities being related. These foreign keys are used to associate records from one entity to records in another entity. Sometimes, the bridge table will also contain additional attributes that are relevant to the relationship itself.

Why Use a Bridge Table?

A direct many-to-many relationship between two entities leads to redundant data and complicated database structures. By introducing a bridge table, we maintain data normalization, reduce redundancy, and simplify querying. It also provides a place to store additional attributes related to the relationship between the two entities.

Example:

Let's consider the case of a **Product** and **Order** relationship. A product can appear in many orders, and an order can contain many products, resulting in a many-to-many relationship.

To resolve this, we introduce a **ProductOrder** bridge table that links **Product** and **Order**. This table will contain:

- **ProductID** (foreign key referencing the **Product** table)

- **OrderID** (foreign key referencing the **Order** table)

Additionally, we may include extra attributes, such as **Quantity** and **Price** to reflect the quantity of each product in the order and the price at the time of purchase.

Bridge Table Example: ProductOrder

ProductOrderID	ProductID	OrderID	Quantity	Price
1	101	5001	2	50
2	102	5002	1	30
3	101	5003	3	50

In this table:

- **ProductID** and **OrderID** act as foreign keys, linking products to orders.

- **Quantity** and **Price** represent additional attributes that are specific to the relationship.

Structure of a Bridge Table

A bridge table typically contains the following elements:

1. **Foreign Keys**: References to the primary keys of the two entities being linked. These foreign keys establish the relationship between the entities.

2. **Additional Attributes**: If there are any attributes that specifically pertain to the relationship itself, they are stored in the bridge table. For example, in a **Student-Course** relationship, you might store **EnrollmentDate** in the bridge table.

3. **Primary Key**: Often, the bridge table uses a composite primary key made up of the two foreign keys, ensuring that each relationship between the two entities is unique.

Practical Considerations

- **Normalization**: The use of bridge tables helps maintain database normalization by avoiding data redundancy. Without a bridge table, the many-to-many relationship would require multiple copies of the same data across multiple tables.

- **Performance**: While bridge tables help normalize data, they can also require more complex queries, as you may need to join multiple tables. Careful indexing and query optimization can mitigate potential performance issues.

Example in a Real-World Scenario:

Consider a **Library** system where **Books** and **Authors** have a many-to-many relationship:

- A book can be written by multiple authors, and an author can write multiple books.

To represent this relationship, a bridge table called **BookAuthor** might be created, containing:

- **BookID** (foreign key referencing **Books**)

- **AuthorID** (foreign key referencing **Authors**)

Additionally, attributes like **ContributionType** (e.g., Primary Author, Co-Author) could be added to capture the role of each author in writing a book.

BookAuthorID	BookID	AuthorID	ContributionType
1	2001	101	Primary Author
2	2001	102	Co-Author
3	2002	101	Co-Author

This bridge table enables the system to efficiently track which authors are associated with which books, without duplicating data or creating complex direct relationships.

Modeling Hierarchies with Self-Joins

In many business scenarios, data entities are organized in a hierarchical structure. For instance, an **Employee** entity might have a hierarchy where employees report to managers, who themselves report to higher-level managers, and so on. These hierarchical relationships are often referred to as **parent-child relationships**, where a parent entity has child entities that are related to it in some way.

In a relational database, one effective way to represent these hierarchical structures is through **self-joins**. A self-join is a join where a table is linked to itself to establish a relationship between rows in the same table.

What is a Self-Join?

A **self-join** involves joining a table with itself by matching a foreign key in one row to a primary key in another row of the same table. This allows us to model parent-child relationships within a single table.

Example: Employee Hierarchy

Consider the **Employee** entity, where each employee reports to a manager. In a relational database, the employee table might look like this:

EmployeeID	EmployeeName	ManagerID
1	John Doe	NULL
2	Jane Smith	1
3	Bob Brown	1
4	Alice White	2
5	Mike Green	2

In this table:

- **EmployeeID** is the primary key.

- **ManagerID** is a foreign key referencing the **EmployeeID** of the employee's manager.

Here, **John Doe** has no manager (represented by NULL), **Jane Smith** and **Bob Brown** report to **John Doe**, and **Alice White** and **Mike Green** report to **Jane Smith**.

To model this hierarchy, we perform a **self-join** on the **Employee** table, where the **ManagerID** in one row is matched to the **EmployeeID** in another row:

```sql
SELECT e.EmployeeName AS Employee, m.EmployeeName AS Manager

FROM Employee e

LEFT JOIN Employee m ON e.ManagerID = m.EmployeeID;
```

The result of this query would look like this:

Employee	Manager
John Doe	NULL
Jane Smith	John Doe
Bob Brown	John Doe
Alice White	Jane Smith
Mike Green	Jane Smith

Michael E. Kirshteyn, Ph.D

This query shows each employee alongside their manager, modeling the hierarchical reporting structure.

Types of Hierarchies

Hierarchical relationships are not limited to employee-manager structures. They can be applied to other types of data as well, such as:

- **Product Categories**: A product may belong to a parent category, and that category may be part of a broader category.

- **Organizational Structures**: Departments can have sub-departments, and each sub-department can have its own hierarchy of teams and employees.

For example, consider the **ProductCategory** table where categories are structured hierarchically:

CategoryID	CategoryName	ParentCategoryID
1	Electronics	NULL
2	Laptops	1
3	Smartphones	1
4	MacBooks	2
5	iPhones	3

In this table, the **ParentCategoryID** is a foreign key that refers to the **CategoryID** of the parent category. A self-join can be used to retrieve the hierarchical structure of categories:

```sql
SELECT c.CategoryName AS SubCategory, p.CategoryName AS ParentCategory
FROM ProductCategory c
LEFT JOIN ProductCategory p ON c.ParentCategoryID = p.CategoryID;
```

This query will output:

SubCategory	ParentCategory
Electronics	NULL
Laptops	Electronics
Smartphones	Electronics
MacBooks	Laptops
iPhones	Smartphones

This self-join effectively models the hierarchy of product categories.

Self-Joins in Practice

When working with hierarchical data, self-joins can be particularly useful for:

- **Employee Reporting Structures**: As seen in the example, employees can be linked to their managers.

- **Product Categories**: Parent-child relationships between categories can be easily represented.

- **Organizational Units**: Departments and sub-departments can be connected using a self-join.

- **Bill of Materials (BOM)**: In manufacturing, a part may consist of other sub-parts, forming a parent-child relationship.

Performance Considerations

While self-joins are useful for modeling hierarchical relationships, they can be performance-intensive, especially with large datasets. Optimizing queries, creating indexes, and ensuring efficient joins can help mitigate performance issues.

Retail Logical Model

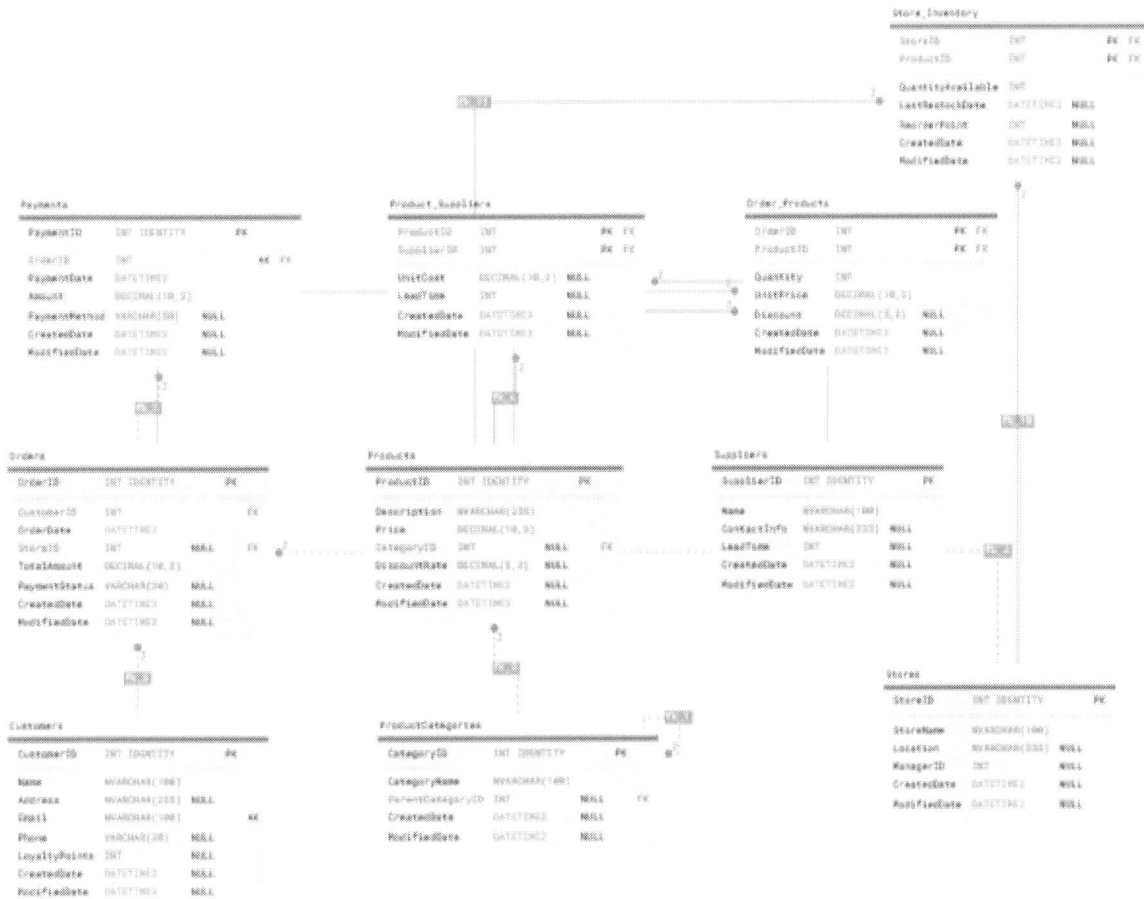

DDL (Data Definition Language) for Retail

-- Create Product Categories table with self-referential relationship

CREATE TABLE ProductCategories (

    CategoryID INT PRIMARY KEY IDENTITY(1,1),

    CategoryName NVARCHAR(100) NOT NULL,

    ParentCategoryID INT,

    CreatedDate DATETIME2 DEFAULT GETDATE(),

    ModifiedDate DATETIME2 DEFAULT GETDATE(),

    FOREIGN KEY (ParentCategoryID) REFERENCES ProductCategories(CategoryID)

Michael E. Kirshteyn, Ph.D

```
);


-- Create Products table

CREATE TABLE Products (

    ProductID INT PRIMARY KEY IDENTITY(1,1),

    Description NVARCHAR(255) NOT NULL,

    Price DECIMAL(10,2) NOT NULL,

    CategoryID INT,

    DiscountRate DECIMAL(5,2),

    CreatedDate DATETIME2 DEFAULT GETDATE(),

    ModifiedDate DATETIME2 DEFAULT GETDATE(),

    FOREIGN KEY (CategoryID) REFERENCES ProductCategories(CategoryID)

);


-- Create Customers table

CREATE TABLE Customers (

    CustomerID INT PRIMARY KEY IDENTITY(1,1),

    Name NVARCHAR(100) NOT NULL,

    Address NVARCHAR(255),

    Email NVARCHAR(100) NOT NULL UNIQUE,

    Phone VARCHAR(20),

    LoyaltyPoints INT DEFAULT 0,

    CreatedDate DATETIME2 DEFAULT GETDATE(),

    ModifiedDate DATETIME2 DEFAULT GETDATE()

);


-- Create Stores table

CREATE TABLE Stores (

    StoreID INT PRIMARY KEY IDENTITY(1,1),

    StoreName NVARCHAR(100) NOT NULL,
```

```
    Location NVARCHAR(255),

    ManagerID INT,

    CreatedDate DATETIME2 DEFAULT GETDATE(),

    ModifiedDate DATETIME2 DEFAULT GETDATE()
);


-- Create Orders table
CREATE TABLE Orders (
    OrderID INT PRIMARY KEY IDENTITY(1,1),

    CustomerID INT NOT NULL,

    OrderDate DATETIME2 NOT NULL DEFAULT GETDATE(),

    StoreID INT,

    TotalAmount DECIMAL(10,2) NOT NULL,

    PaymentStatus VARCHAR(20) CHECK (PaymentStatus IN ('Pending', 'Completed', 'Failed')),

    CreatedDate DATETIME2 DEFAULT GETDATE(),

    ModifiedDate DATETIME2 DEFAULT GETDATE(),

    FOREIGN KEY (CustomerID) REFERENCES Customers(CustomerID),

    FOREIGN KEY (StoreID) REFERENCES Stores(StoreID)
);


-- Create Payments table
CREATE TABLE Payments (
    PaymentID INT PRIMARY KEY IDENTITY(1,1),

    OrderID INT NOT NULL UNIQUE,

    PaymentDate DATETIME2 NOT NULL DEFAULT GETDATE(),

    Amount DECIMAL(10,2) NOT NULL,

    PaymentMethod VARCHAR(50),

    CreatedDate DATETIME2 DEFAULT GETDATE(),

    ModifiedDate DATETIME2 DEFAULT GETDATE(),

    FOREIGN KEY (OrderID) REFERENCES Orders(OrderID)
```

```sql
);


-- Create Suppliers table
CREATE TABLE Suppliers (
    SupplierID INT PRIMARY KEY IDENTITY(1,1),
    Name NVARCHAR(100) NOT NULL,
    ContactInfo NVARCHAR(255),
    LeadTime INT, -- In days
    CreatedDate DATETIME2 DEFAULT GETDATE(),
    ModifiedDate DATETIME2 DEFAULT GETDATE()
);


-- Create Product_Suppliers bridge table
CREATE TABLE Product_Suppliers (
    ProductID INT,
    SupplierID INT,
    UnitCost DECIMAL(10,2),
    LeadTime INT, -- In days
    CreatedDate DATETIME2 DEFAULT GETDATE(),
    ModifiedDate DATETIME2 DEFAULT GETDATE(),
    PRIMARY KEY (ProductID, SupplierID),
    FOREIGN KEY (ProductID) REFERENCES Products(ProductID),
    FOREIGN KEY (SupplierID) REFERENCES Suppliers(SupplierID)
);


-- Create Order_Products bridge table
CREATE TABLE Order_Products (
    OrderID INT,
    ProductID INT,
    Quantity INT NOT NULL,
```

```
    UnitPrice DECIMAL(10,2) NOT NULL,

    Discount DECIMAL(5,2) DEFAULT 0,

    CreatedDate DATETIME2 DEFAULT GETDATE(),

    ModifiedDate DATETIME2 DEFAULT GETDATE(),

    PRIMARY KEY (OrderID, ProductID),

    FOREIGN KEY (OrderID) REFERENCES Orders(OrderID),

    FOREIGN KEY (ProductID) REFERENCES Products(ProductID)

);


-- Create Store_Inventory bridge table
CREATE TABLE Store_Inventory (

    StoreID INT,

    ProductID INT,

    QuantityAvailable INT NOT NULL DEFAULT 0,

    LastRestockDate DATETIME2,

    ReorderPoint INT,

    CreatedDate DATETIME2 DEFAULT GETDATE(),

    ModifiedDate DATETIME2 DEFAULT GETDATE(),

    PRIMARY KEY (StoreID, ProductID),

    FOREIGN KEY (StoreID) REFERENCES Stores(StoreID),

    FOREIGN KEY (ProductID) REFERENCES Products(ProductID)

);


-- Create indexes for better performance
CREATE INDEX IX_Products_Category ON Products(CategoryID);

CREATE INDEX IX_Orders_Customer ON Orders(CustomerID);

CREATE INDEX IX_Orders_Store ON Orders(StoreID);

CREATE INDEX IX_OrderProducts_Product ON Order_Products(ProductID);

CREATE INDEX IX_StoreInventory_Product ON Store_Inventory(ProductID);

CREATE INDEX IX_ProductSuppliers_Supplier ON Product_Suppliers(SupplierID);
```

```
CREATE INDEX IX_ProductCategories_Parent ON ProductCategories(ParentCategoryID);


-- Create trigger for maintaining ModifiedDate
CREATE TRIGGER TR_Products_Update ON Products
AFTER UPDATE AS
BEGIN
    UPDATE Products
    SET ModifiedDate = GETDATE()
    FROM Products p
    INNER JOIN inserted i ON p.ProductID = i.ProductID;
END;


-- Create view for inventory status
CREATE VIEW vw_InventoryStatus AS
SELECT
    p.ProductID,
    p.Description,
    s.StoreID,
    s.StoreName,
    si.QuantityAvailable,
    si.LastRestockDate,
    si.ReorderPoint
FROM Products p
JOIN Store_Inventory si ON p.ProductID = si.ProductID
JOIN Stores s ON si.StoreID = s.StoreID;


-- Create view for sales analysis
CREATE VIEW vw_SalesAnalysis AS
SELECT
    p.ProductID,
```

```
    p.Description,

    c.CategoryName,

    COUNT(DISTINCT o.OrderID) as TotalOrders,

    SUM(op.Quantity) as TotalQuantitySold,

    SUM(op.Quantity * op.UnitPrice) as TotalRevenue

FROM Products p

JOIN ProductCategories c ON p.CategoryID = c.CategoryID

JOIN Order_Products op ON p.ProductID = op.ProductID

JOIN Orders o ON op.OrderID = o.OrderID

GROUP BY p.ProductID, p.Description, c.CategoryName;
```

Exercise: Relationship Derivation and Primary Key Selection

Exercise Instructions:

1. Given the following scenario: A customer places an order at a store and makes a payment. Identify the entities involved and the relationships between them.

2. Derive the primary keys for each entity. Ensure that each entity has a unique identifier.

3. Determine the cardinality of the relationships and explain your reasoning.

Case Study: E-Commerce Retailer Data Model

An e-commerce retailer sells products online and ships them directly to customers. The retailer wants to create a data model that accurately represents its operations.

Entities Involved:

- **Product**: ProductID, Description, Price, Category, StockLevel

- **Customer**: CustomerID, Name, Address, Email, OrderHistory

- **Order**: OrderID, CustomerID, OrderDate, TotalAmount, PaymentStatus

- **Payment**: PaymentID, OrderID, PaymentDate, Amount, PaymentMethod

- **Inventory**: ProductID, QuantityInStock, WarehouseLocation

- **Supplier**: SupplierID, Name, ContactInfo

Relationships:

- A **Customer** places multiple **Orders** (1:M).

- An **Order** contains multiple **Products** (M:M).

- A **Product** is supplied by a **Supplier** (M:1).

- A **Payment** corresponds to an **Order** (1:1).

- **Inventory** tracks **Product** quantities in **Warehouses** (M:1).

This case study demonstrates how an e-commerce retailer's operations can be modeled using entities and relationships, allowing for better management of sales, inventory, and customer interactions.

Chapter Summary and Quiz

In this chapter, we explored data modeling for the retail industry, focusing on key concepts such as entities, attributes, relationships, and cardinality. We identified essential components of a retail data model, including sales, inventory, and customer management. Through an exercise and case study, we demonstrated how to construct a conceptual model and break it down into subject areas. Finally, we discussed the importance of understanding relationships and primary keys in creating an effective data model.

Quiz:

1. What are the key components of a retail data model?

2. Define the relationships between the entities **Customer**, **Order**, and **Payment**.

3. What are the benefits of dividing a retail data model into subject areas like Sales, Inventory, and Customer Management?

4. How do cardinality and relationships help ensure data integrity in a retail data model?

5. In the case study, what were the key entities and relationships for the e-commerce retailer?

This concludes Chapter 2. Be sure to review the concepts, complete the exercises, and test your understanding with the

Chapter 3: Data Modeling for the Manufacturing Industry

Industry Overview: Key Processes and Data Flows

The manufacturing industry is a critical sector that involves the production of goods through the transformation of raw materials, components, or parts into finished products. This process often involves complex workflows, resource management, and coordination between various stakeholders, including suppliers, manufacturers, distributors, and customers.

Key processes in manufacturing include:

- **Production**: The conversion of raw materials and components into finished products through various processes like assembly, machining, and quality control.

- **Supply Chain Management**: The management of suppliers, raw materials, and logistics to ensure that production schedules are met.

- **Inventory Management**: The tracking and management of raw materials, work-in-progress, and finished goods to maintain production efficiency and prevent stockouts.

- **Orders and Fulfillment**: The handling of customer orders and ensuring that the right products are delivered on time.

The data flows in a manufacturing environment typically involve tracking the movement of materials, components, and products throughout the production process. Key data elements include:

- **Products**: Details about the items being manufactured, including parts, materials, and finished goods.

- **Suppliers**: Information about vendors providing raw materials, components, or services.

- **Production Orders**: Requests for manufacturing that specify what needs to be produced, in what quantity, and by when.

- **Inventory**: Data on the availability of raw materials, components, and finished products.

- **Work Orders**: Specific instructions detailing the work to be done on a production line or workstation.

- **Sales Orders**: Customer orders that specify the products and quantities requested.

Manufacturing Components: Products, Suppliers, Orders, Inventory

A manufacturing data model involves key components that represent the core entities in the manufacturing process. Below are the essential components of a manufacturing data model:

- **Product**: Represents the goods that are produced, whether they are raw materials, components, or finished products.

  - Attributes: ProductID (PK), ProductName, Description, Category, Cost, Price, SupplierID (FK)

- **Supplier**: Represents the vendors or companies that provide raw materials, components, or subassemblies for the manufacturing process.

  - Attributes: SupplierID (PK), Name, ContactInfo, LeadTime

- **Production Order**: Represents a request to produce a certain quantity of products. This includes details on the product, quantity, and deadlines.

  - Attributes: OrderID (PK), ProductID (FK), Quantity, ScheduledStartDate, ScheduledEndDate, Status

- **Work Order**: Represents specific tasks or instructions related to the production process, often associated with machinery, labor, or assembly processes.

  - Attributes: WorkOrderID (PK), ProductionOrderID (FK), WorkStationID, Quantity, Status

- **Inventory**: Represents the storage of raw materials, components, or finished goods in warehouses or production areas.

  - Attributes: ProductID (FK), WarehouseID (FK), QuantityAvailable, QuantityOnOrder, MinimumStockLevel

- **Warehouse**: Represents the physical locations where materials and products are stored.

  - Attributes: WarehouseID (PK), Location, ManagerID

- **Sales Order**: Represents customer orders for finished products.

  - Attributes: SalesOrderID (PK), CustomerID (FK), ProductID (FK), Quantity, OrderDate, ShipDate

Creating the Conceptual Model for Manufacturing

The conceptual model is the first step in developing a detailed data model and focuses on identifying the core entities and relationships. The goal of this phase is to create a high-level view of the manufacturing business and capture the main data flows.

Michael E. Kirshteyn, Ph.D

For manufacturing, the conceptual model would include the following:

1. **Entities**: Product, Supplier, Production Order, Work Order, Inventory, Warehouse, Sales Order.

2. **Relationships**:

   - A **Supplier** provides multiple **Products** (1:M relationship).

   - A **Production Order** creates multiple **Work Orders** (1:M relationship).

   - A **Product** is part of multiple **Production Orders** (M:M relationship).

   - **Inventory** tracks **Products** at **Warehouses** (M:1 relationship).

   - A **Sales Order** requests a **Product** (M:1 relationship).

3. **Primary Keys**: Each entity will have a unique primary key, such as `ProductID`, `SupplierID`, `OrderID`, etc., to uniquely identify each record.

At this stage, the primary focus is on establishing the relationships and ensuring that the model captures the essential business processes.

Breaking Down the Model into Subject Areas: Production, Supply Chain, Inventory Management

To better organize a manufacturing data model, we break it down into subject areas. Each subject area represents a key part of the manufacturing process.

1. **Production**: This subject area handles all aspects of creating the product, from the creation of production orders to the generation of work orders and completion of products.

   - Key entities: Production Order, Work Order, Product, Warehouse

   - Example: A production order is created for a specific product, which is then broken down into work orders across different workstations.

2. **Supply Chain**: This subject area tracks the procurement and delivery of materials from suppliers to the manufacturing facility.

   - Key entities: Supplier, Product, Purchase Order

   - Example: A supplier provides components to fulfill a production order for a specific product.

3. **Inventory Management**: This subject area focuses on tracking the availability of raw materials, work-in-progress items, and finished goods.

   - Key entities: Product, Inventory, Warehouse

   - Example: Raw materials are stored in the warehouse, and inventory levels are updated as products are produced or shipped.

Setting Cardinality and Analyzing Relationships

The relationships between entities in a manufacturing data model must be clearly defined to ensure data integrity and accuracy. Understanding cardinality helps in correctly linking entities.

1. **Supplier to Product**: One-to-many (1:M). A supplier can provide multiple products, but each product is sourced from only one supplier.

2. **Production Order to Work Order**: One-to-many (1:M). Each production order can generate multiple work orders, but each work order is tied to a specific production order.

3. **Product to Sales Order**: Many-to-one (M:1). A product can be included in multiple sales orders, but each sales order refers to one specific product.

4. **Inventory to Product**: One-to-many (1:M). A product can have multiple inventory records at different warehouses, but each inventory record is linked to only one product.

These relationships ensure that the data model accurately reflects the real-world processes and interactions within a manufacturing business.

Manufacturing Logical Model

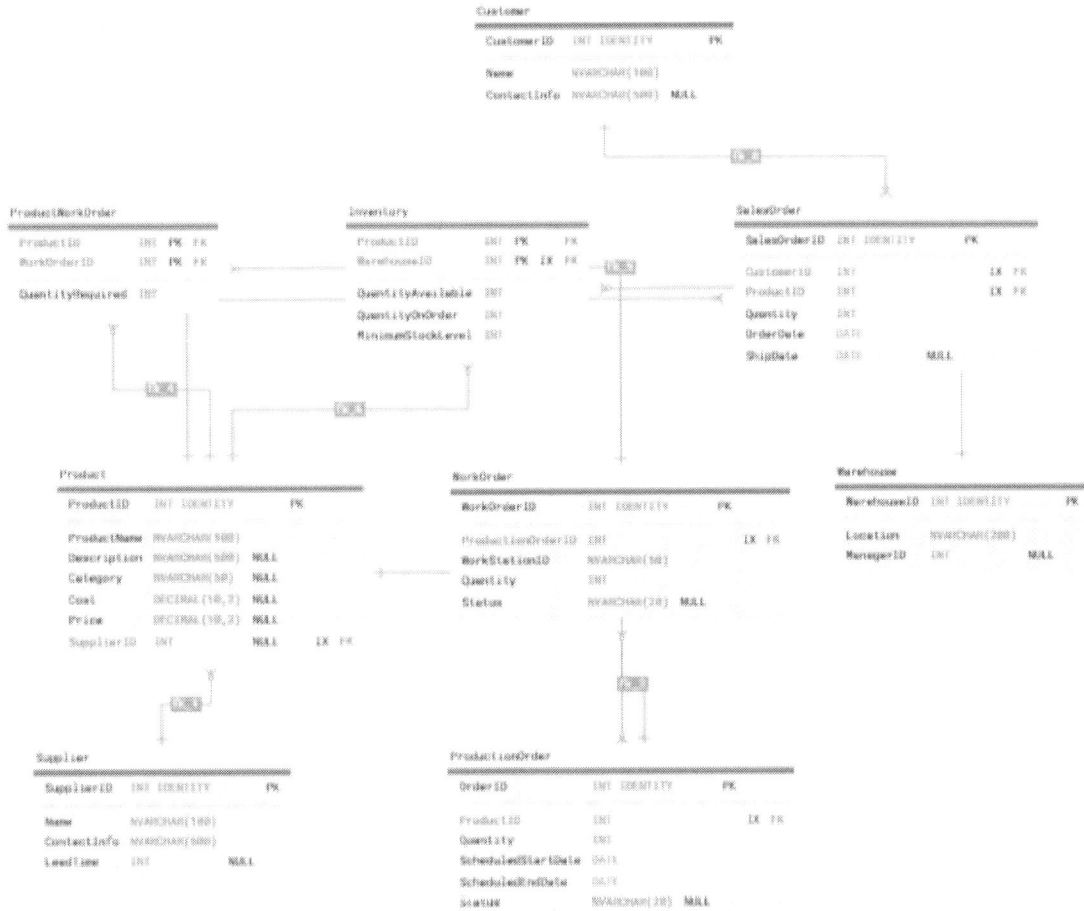

DDL for Manufacturing

-- Create tables for Manufacturing Database

-- Supplier table

```
CREATE TABLE Supplier (
    SupplierID INT PRIMARY KEY IDENTITY(1,1),
    Name NVARCHAR(100) NOT NULL,
    ContactInfo NVARCHAR(500) NOT NULL,
```

```
    LeadTime INT -- in days
);


-- Product table
CREATE TABLE Product (
    ProductID INT PRIMARY KEY IDENTITY(1,1),
    ProductName NVARCHAR(100) NOT NULL,
    Description NVARCHAR(500),
    Category NVARCHAR(50),
    Cost DECIMAL(10,2),
    Price DECIMAL(10,2),
    SupplierID INT,
    FOREIGN KEY (SupplierID) REFERENCES Supplier(SupplierID)
);


-- Warehouse table
CREATE TABLE Warehouse (
    WarehouseID INT PRIMARY KEY IDENTITY(1,1),
    Location NVARCHAR(200) NOT NULL,
    ManagerID INT
);


-- Customer table (needed for Sales Orders)
CREATE TABLE Customer (
    CustomerID INT PRIMARY KEY IDENTITY(1,1),
    Name NVARCHAR(100) NOT NULL,
    ContactInfo NVARCHAR(500)
);


-- Production Order table
```

```
CREATE TABLE ProductionOrder (

    OrderID INT PRIMARY KEY IDENTITY(1,1),

    ProductID INT NOT NULL,

    Quantity INT NOT NULL,

    ScheduledStartDate DATE NOT NULL,

    ScheduledEndDate DATE NOT NULL,

    Status NVARCHAR(20) CHECK (Status IN ('Pending', 'In Progress', 'Completed', 'Cancelled')),

    FOREIGN KEY (ProductID) REFERENCES Product(ProductID)

);


-- Work Order table
CREATE TABLE WorkOrder (

    WorkOrderID INT PRIMARY KEY IDENTITY(1,1),

    ProductionOrderID INT NOT NULL,

    WorkStationID NVARCHAR(50) NOT NULL,

    Quantity INT NOT NULL,

    Status NVARCHAR(20) CHECK (Status IN ('Pending', 'In Progress', 'Completed', 'Cancelled')),

    FOREIGN KEY (ProductionOrderID) REFERENCES ProductionOrder(OrderID)

);


-- Bridge table for Product-WorkOrder many-to-many relationship
CREATE TABLE ProductWorkOrder (

    ProductID INT NOT NULL,

    WorkOrderID INT NOT NULL,

    QuantityRequired INT NOT NULL,

    PRIMARY KEY (ProductID, WorkOrderID),

    FOREIGN KEY (ProductID) REFERENCES Product(ProductID),

    FOREIGN KEY (WorkOrderID) REFERENCES WorkOrder(WorkOrderID)

);
```

```sql
-- Inventory table
CREATE TABLE Inventory (
    ProductID INT NOT NULL,
    WarehouseID INT NOT NULL,
    QuantityAvailable INT NOT NULL,
    QuantityOnOrder INT NOT NULL,
    MinimumStockLevel INT NOT NULL,
    PRIMARY KEY (ProductID, WarehouseID),
    FOREIGN KEY (ProductID) REFERENCES Product(ProductID),
    FOREIGN KEY (WarehouseID) REFERENCES Warehouse(WarehouseID)
);

-- Sales Order table
CREATE TABLE SalesOrder (
    SalesOrderID INT PRIMARY KEY IDENTITY(1,1),
    CustomerID INT NOT NULL,
    ProductID INT NOT NULL,
    Quantity INT NOT NULL,
    OrderDate DATE NOT NULL,
    ShipDate DATE,
    FOREIGN KEY (CustomerID) REFERENCES Customer(CustomerID),
    FOREIGN KEY (ProductID) REFERENCES Product(ProductID)
);

-- Add indexes for performance
CREATE INDEX IX_Product_SupplierID ON Product(SupplierID);
CREATE INDEX IX_ProductionOrder_ProductID ON ProductionOrder(ProductID);
CREATE INDEX IX_WorkOrder_ProductionOrderID ON WorkOrder(ProductionOrderID);
CREATE INDEX IX_Inventory_WarehouseID ON Inventory(WarehouseID);
CREATE INDEX IX_SalesOrder_CustomerID ON SalesOrder(CustomerID);
```

CREATE INDEX IX_SalesOrder_ProductID ON SalesOrder(ProductID);

Exercise: Identifying and Defining Manufacturing Relationships

Exercise Instructions:

1. Consider a scenario in which a manufacturer receives an order from a customer, creates a production order to produce the required products, and manages the inventory of raw materials needed for production.

2. Identify the key entities involved and define the relationships between them.

3. For each relationship, define the cardinality (e.g., 1:M, M:1) and explain why that cardinality is appropriate for the scenario.

Case Study: Data Model for a Multi-Product Manufacturing Company

A multi-product manufacturing company produces a wide range of products, including electronics, automotive parts, and consumer goods. The company sources materials from various suppliers and ships products to customers globally.

Entities Involved:

- **Product**: ProductID, ProductName, Description, Category, SupplierID (FK)

- **Supplier**: SupplierID, Name, ContactInfo

- **Production Order**: OrderID, ProductID (FK), Quantity, StartDate, EndDate

- **Work Order**: WorkOrderID, ProductionOrderID (FK), WorkStation, Quantity, Status

- **Inventory**: ProductID, WarehouseID, QuantityAvailable

- **Sales Order**: SalesOrderID, ProductID (FK), Quantity, CustomerID (FK), OrderDate

Relationships:

- A **Supplier** provides multiple **Products** (1:M).

- A **Production Order** is associated with multiple **Work Orders** (1:M).

- A **Product** is manufactured through multiple **Work Orders** (M:M).

- **Inventory** tracks the availability of **Products** at different **Warehouses** (M:1).

- A **Sales Order** is placed by a **Customer** for a **Product** (M:1).

In this case study, we demonstrate how a manufacturing company with a broad product line can utilize a data model to manage its production, supply chain, and sales operations.

Chapter Summary and Quiz

In this chapter, we explored the core aspects of data modeling for the manufacturing industry. We examined key components like products, suppliers, production orders, and inventory, and created a conceptual model that captures the relationships between these entities. We also broke the model down into subject areas such as production, supply chain, and inventory management, and analyzed the cardinality and relationships to ensure data accuracy.

Quiz:

1. What are the main components of a manufacturing data model?

2. How does the **Production Order** relate to the **Work Order** in the manufacturing process?

3. Explain the cardinality of the relationship between **Product** and **Supplier**.

4. What subject areas should be included in a manufacturing data model, and why are they important?

5. In the case study, what key entities were used to manage the manufacturing process?

This concludes Chapter 3. Be sure to review the concepts, complete the exercises, and test your understanding with the quiz. Next, we'll move into industry-specific examples for other sectors.

Chapter 4: Data Modeling for the Healthcare Industry

Overview of Healthcare Data Needs and Regulations

The healthcare industry relies on comprehensive data management to improve patient care, ensure accuracy, and streamline operations. Data modeling in healthcare must account for strict data privacy regulations, such as HIPAA in the United States, which protect patient information. Additionally, healthcare data models often involve complex relationships due to varied data types and the need for interoperability across diverse systems, such as electronic health records (EHR), billing systems, and lab information systems (LIS). Understanding healthcare's unique data needs and regulatory landscape is foundational to effective data modeling in this industry.

Key Entities: Patients, Providers, Treatments, Billing

In healthcare data models, several core entities are central to representing patient interactions, medical services, and billing processes:

- **Patients**: The primary entity in healthcare, representing individuals receiving medical care. Key attributes may include PatientID, Name, Date of Birth, Contact Information, and Medical History.

- **Providers**: Entities that represent healthcare professionals and institutions, including doctors, nurses, and hospitals. Attributes often include ProviderID, Name, Specialty, and Affiliated Hospital.

- **Treatments**: Represents medical services and procedures provided to patients. Attributes might include TreatmentID, TreatmentType, Date, and Outcome.

- **Billing**: Captures the financial transactions associated with healthcare services, tracking costs and payment details. Common attributes are BillingID, PatientID, ProviderID, TreatmentID, Cost, and PaymentStatus.

These entities work together to capture a patient's journey through the healthcare system, from diagnosis to treatment to billing.

Constructing a Healthcare Conceptual Model

The conceptual model in healthcare data modeling provides a high-level view of how the main entities interact without diving into specific details. This model serves as a foundational framework to guide the logical and physical models. Here's an example of how the core entities relate to each other:

- **Patient - Provider Relationship**: Patients are assigned to Providers, where each patient typically has one primary provider but may receive care from multiple specialists over time.

- **Patient - Treatment Relationship**: Patients undergo various Treatments, each associated with specific healthcare providers.

- **Provider - Treatment Relationship**: Providers administer or oversee Treatments, linking patient care directly to the healthcare professionals responsible.

- **Patient - Billing Relationship**: Each patient's treatments and services generate Billing records, tracking the costs, payments, and outstanding balances.

This conceptual model captures the core interactions in healthcare, illustrating the flow from patient care to financial processing.

Subject Area Breakdown: Patient Management, Treatment Records, Billing

In a healthcare logical data model, it's beneficial to divide data into subject areas. This section outlines key subject areas that facilitate focused and organized data modeling.

1. **Patient Management**: This subject area includes details about patients, their personal and demographic information, medical history, and insurance data. Entities in this area may include Patient, InsurancePlan, and PatientHistory.

2. **Treatment Records**: Captures details of the medical services provided. This subject area tracks the treatments and procedures patients receive, the providers who administer them, and any associated diagnoses. Entities include Treatment, Diagnosis, Procedure, and Provider.

3. **Billing**: Manages financial aspects of healthcare, including costs, payments, and insurance claims. Key entities in this subject area are Billing, InsuranceClaim, and Payment, linked to patients, treatments, and insurance plans.

Cardinality and Complex Relationships in Healthcare

Healthcare data models often include complex relationships and cardinalities due to the intricacy of patient care, treatment processes, and provider interactions. Here are some examples of relationships with cardinality considerations:

- **One-to-Many (1:M)**: A Patient may have multiple Treatments, but each Treatment is for a single Patient.

- **Many-to-One (M:1)**: Multiple Treatments may involve the same Provider, as a single doctor can treat many patients.

- **Many-to-Many (M:N)**: Patients can consult multiple Providers, and Providers can treat multiple Patients. This relationship is often resolved through a junction entity, such as PatientProviderAssignment.

In healthcare, these relationships can grow more complex with additional variables like insurance data and referrals, making it crucial to accurately represent cardinality and associations for reliable data analysis and reporting.

Logical Data Model for the Healthcare Industry

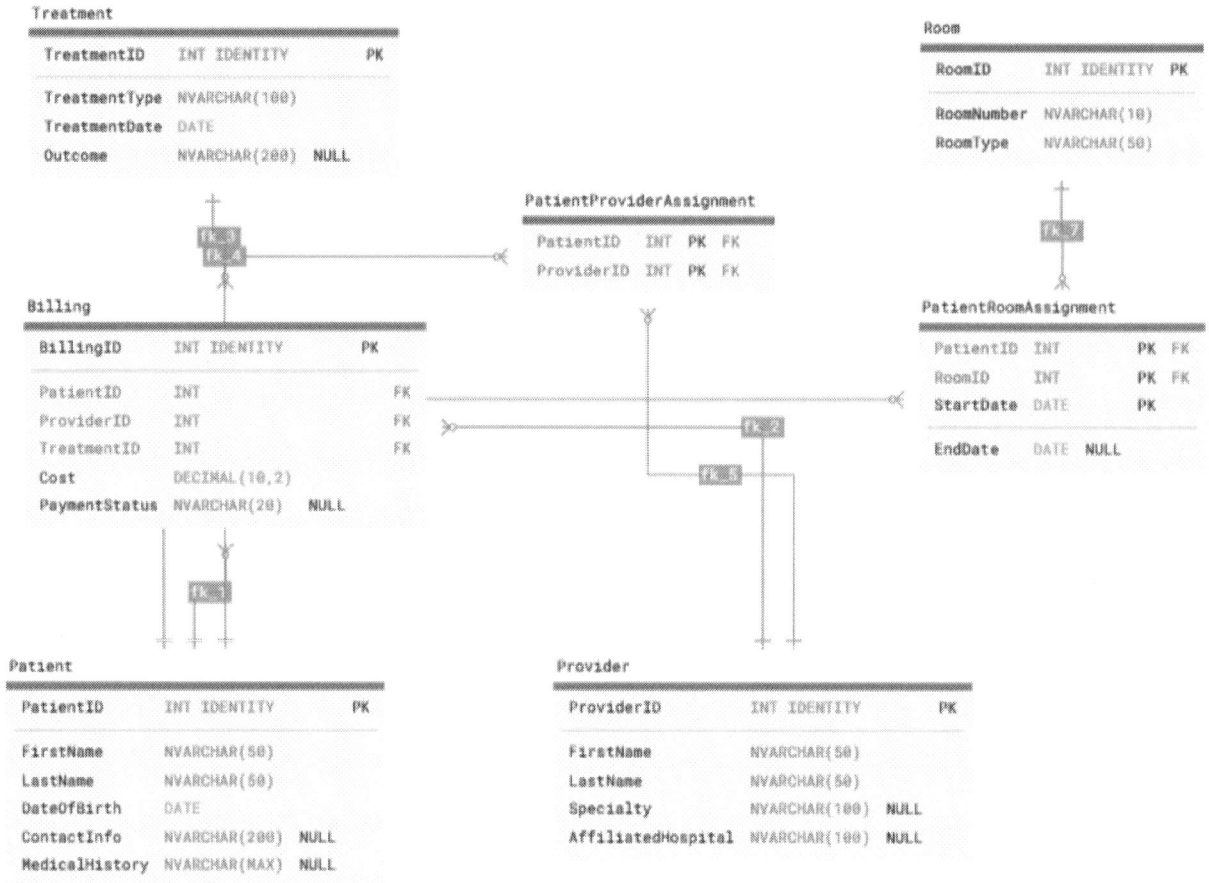

DDL for Healthcare Industry

-- Patient table

CREATE TABLE Patient (

   PatientID INT PRIMARY KEY IDENTITY(1,1),

   FirstName NVARCHAR(50) NOT NULL,

   LastName NVARCHAR(50) NOT NULL,

   DateOfBirth DATE NOT NULL,

   ContactInfo NVARCHAR(200),

   MedicalHistory NVARCHAR(MAX)

);

-- Provider table

```
CREATE TABLE Provider (
    ProviderID INT PRIMARY KEY IDENTITY(1,1),
    FirstName NVARCHAR(50) NOT NULL,
    LastName NVARCHAR(50) NOT NULL,
    Spccialty NVARCHAR(100),
    AffiliatedHospital NVARCHAR(100)
);
```

-- Treatment table

```
CREATE TABLE Treatment (
    TreatmentID INT PRIMARY KEY IDENTITY(1,1),
    TreatmentType NVARCHAR(100) NOT NULL,
    TreatmentDate DATE NOT NULL,
    Outcome NVARCHAR(200)
);
```

-- Billing table

```
CREATE TABLE Billing (
    BillingID INT PRIMARY KEY IDENTITY(1,1),
    PatientID INT NOT NULL,
    ProviderID INT NOT NULL,
    TreatmentID INT NOT NULL,
    Cost DECIMAL(10,2) NOT NULL,
    PaymentStatus NVARCHAR(20) CHECK (PaymentStatus IN ('Pending', 'Paid', 'Denied')),
    FOREIGN KEY (PatientID) REFERENCES Patient(PatientID),
    FOREIGN KEY (ProviderID) REFERENCES Provider(ProviderID),
    FOREIGN KEY (TreatmentID) REFERENCES Treatment(TreatmentID)
```

```sql
);


-- Bridge table for Patient-Provider many-to-many relationship
CREATE TABLE PatientProviderAssignment (
    PatientID INT NOT NULL,
    ProviderID INT NOT NULL,
    PRIMARY KEY (PatientID, ProviderID),
    FOREIGN KEY (PatientID) REFERENCES Patient(PatientID),
    FOREIGN KEY (ProviderID) REFERENCES Provider(ProviderID)
);


-- Room table
CREATE TABLE Room (
    RoomID INT PRIMARY KEY IDENTITY(1,1),
    RoomNumber NVARCHAR(10) NOT NULL,
    RoomType NVARCHAR(50) NOT NULL
);


-- Patient Room Assignment table
CREATE TABLE PatientRoomAssignment (
    PatientID INT NOT NULL,
    RoomID INT NOT NULL,
    StartDate DATE NOT NULL,
    EndDate DATE,
    PRIMARY KEY (PatientID, RoomID, StartDate),
    FOREIGN KEY (PatientID) REFERENCES Patient(PatientID),
    FOREIGN KEY (RoomID) REFERENCES Room(RoomID)
);
```

-- Add indexes for performance

CREATE INDEX IX_Billing_PatientID ON Billing(PatientID);

CREATE INDEX IX_Billing_ProviderID ON Billing(ProviderID);

CREATE INDEX IX_Billing_TreatmentID ON Billing(TreatmentID);

CREATE INDEX IX_PatientProviderAssignment_PatientID ON PatientProviderAssignment(PatientID);

CREATE INDEX IX_PatientProviderAssignment_ProviderID ON PatientProviderAssignment(ProviderID);

CREATE INDEX IX_PatientRoomAssignment_PatientID ON PatientRoomAssignment(PatientID);

CREATE INDEX IX_PatientRoomAssignment_RoomID ON PatientRoomAssignment(RoomID);

Exercise: Modeling Patient-Provider and Treatment Relationships

Objective: Create a data model diagram that illustrates the relationships among Patients, Providers, and Treatments.

1. Identify the entities involved in the patient-provider-treatment cycle, including Patient, Provider, Treatment, and Billing.

2. Define attributes for each entity based on healthcare needs (e.g., PatientID, ProviderID, TreatmentDate, etc.).

3. Map out the relationships:

  - **Patient to Provider**: Many-to-Many (a patient can have multiple providers, and a provider can treat multiple patients).

  - **Patient to Treatment**: One-to-Many (a patient may receive multiple treatments).

  - **Provider to Treatment**: One-to-Many (a provider may oversee multiple treatments).

4. Draw a diagram (using Lucidchart or ERwin) showing these entities, attributes, and relationships.

This exercise will help you understand how to represent core healthcare relationships and cardinality within a logical data model.

Case Study: Hospital Patient and Treatment Data Model

In this case study, we'll examine how a hospital manages its patient and treatment data. This model includes entities for Patient, Provider, Treatment, Room, and Billing to support patient management, clinical care, and financial processing. Key aspects include:

1. **Patient-Provider Assignments**: Represents the many-to-many relationship between patients and providers, allowing each patient to be treated by multiple providers while each provider cares for multiple patients.

2. **Room Assignments**: Tracks which room a patient occupies during their stay, allowing for 1:M relationships where a single room can host multiple patients over time but only one patient at a time.

3. **Billing Process**: Includes entities for Billing and Payment linked to Treatment and Patient records, capturing costs for each treatment and patient payment history.

4. **Treatment History**: Tracks each patient's treatment records with details on the provider, date, and treatment type, allowing the hospital to maintain comprehensive patient histories.

Chapter Summary and Quiz

In this chapter, we covered the following topics:

- The specific data needs and regulatory considerations in healthcare, with an emphasis on HIPAA.

- Key entities such as Patients, Providers, Treatments, and Billing.

- How to construct a conceptual model and break down data into subject areas for Patient Management, Treatment Records, and Billing.

- Important cardinality and complex relationships specific to healthcare, such as the patient-provider and patient-treatment relationships.

- A hands-on exercise to model these relationships and a case study of a hospital's data model.

Quiz:

1. What is the significance of regulatory requirements like HIPAA in healthcare data modeling?

2. List and describe the core entities commonly found in a healthcare data model.

3. Explain the many-to-many relationship between Patients and Providers. How can this relationship be modeled in a logical data model?

4. Why is it beneficial to break down a healthcare data model into subject areas?

5. In the context of billing, what entities are typically linked to track payments and insurance claims?

This concludes Chapter 4. With a solid foundation in healthcare data modeling, you'll be well-prepared to tackle more specialized industries and explore how different sectors adapt data modeling principles to their unique requirements.

Chapter 5: Data Modeling for the Insurance Industry

Insurance Industry Overview: Data Flows and Regulatory Considerations

The insurance industry involves complex data flows that span from policy issuance to claims processing, with extensive regulatory considerations to ensure consumer protection and data integrity. Insurers handle sensitive customer data, as well as financial and contractual details related to policies and claims, often regulated by laws like GDPR in Europe and the NAIC Model Laws in the U.S. These regulations mandate strict protocols for data privacy, security, and retention, shaping how data models are structured. A well-designed insurance data model provides clarity, accuracy, and traceability, ensuring compliance and supporting streamlined business operations.

Core Insurance Entities: Policies, Clients, Claims, Premiums

Insurance data models often revolve around several core entities that form the foundation for handling client accounts, policies, and claims processing:

- **Policies**: Represents insurance contracts between the insurer and the client, defining coverage types, terms, and policy start/end dates. Key attributes include PolicyID, CoverageType, PolicyEffectiveDate, and PremiumAmount.

- **Clients**: The individuals or organizations holding insurance policies. Client attributes may include ClientID, Name, Contact Information, and Risk Profile.

- **Claims**: Documents requests by clients to receive benefits or compensation based on policy terms. Claim attributes include ClaimID, ClaimDate, ClaimStatus, and ClaimAmount.

- **Premiums**: Represents the periodic payment clients make to maintain their policies. Attributes include PremiumID, PaymentDate, Amount, and PaymentStatus.

These entities allow insurers to manage essential aspects of their business, from underwriting and policy administration to claims processing and premium collections.

Building the Insurance Conceptual Model

A conceptual data model in the insurance industry highlights the core relationships between clients, policies, claims, and premiums without delving into technical details. This model gives an overview of the insurance workflow, from client policy creation to claims and payments, and supports logical data model development.

Key relationships in a conceptual insurance model include:

- **Client - Policy Relationship**: A one-to-many relationship, where a client may hold multiple policies, but each policy belongs to a single client.

- **Policy - Claim Relationship**: A one-to-many relationship, as a policy can have multiple claims filed against it, but each claim is linked to only one policy.

- **Client - Premium Relationship**: Another one-to-many relationship, where a client makes multiple premium payments to keep a policy active, and each premium payment is linked to one client and one policy.

This conceptual model sets the stage for defining detailed entities and relationships in the logical data model.

Subject Areas: Client Management, Policy Administration, Claims Processing

Organizing data models into subject areas provides structure and clarity, making it easier to manage and maintain insurance data. Below are some core subject areas for insurance:

1. **Client Management**: Covers client demographics, contact details, and risk information. Important entities include Client, Address, RiskAssessment, and ContactHistory.

2. **Policy Administration**: Involves data related to insurance policy details, terms, and payment schedules. Entities may include Policy, Coverage, Premium, and PaymentSchedule.

3. **Claims Processing**: Focuses on managing claims data, from claim creation to resolution. Key entities are Claim, ClaimDetails, Policy, and Settlement.

These subject areas provide a framework for representing the insurance lifecycle, ensuring that client, policy, and claim data are organized in a logical and efficient manner.

Defining Relationships and Cardinality in Insurance Models

Insurance models involve various relationships, each with specific cardinalities. Below are examples of how these relationships are typically structured:

- **Client to Policy (1:M)**: A client may hold multiple policies, but each policy is owned by only one client.

- **Policy to Claim (1:M)**: Each policy may have multiple claims filed over time, representing a one-to-many relationship.

- **Policy to Premium (1:M)**: Each policy has multiple premiums (payments) associated with it, where a premium payment schedule ensures continued coverage.

- **Claim to Settlement (1:1)**: Once a claim is processed, it often results in a single settlement payment or denial, forming a one-to-one relationship between Claim and Settlement.

Understanding these relationships and cardinalities is essential in structuring a comprehensive and compliant insurance data model.

Exercise: Primary Key Selection and Relationship Derivation

Objective: Develop a data model for insurance claims, focusing on primary key selection and relationship derivation.

1. **Identify entities**: Begin with core entities, including Client, Policy, Claim, and Premium.

2. **Define primary keys**: Assign unique identifiers such as ClientID, PolicyID, ClaimID, and PremiumID.

3. **Derive relationships**: Use the following relationships to connect entities:

  - **Client - Policy**: 1:M, where each client has multiple policies.

  - **Policy - Claim**: 1:M, where each policy can have multiple claims.

  - **Policy - Premium**: 1:M, where each policy requires multiple premium payments.

4. **Diagram the model**: Using Lucidchart or ERwin, create a visual representation of these relationships, ensuring cardinality is accurately represented.

This exercise highlights how primary keys and relationships create a foundational structure for insurance data models.

Insurance Provider Logical Data Model for Claims Processing

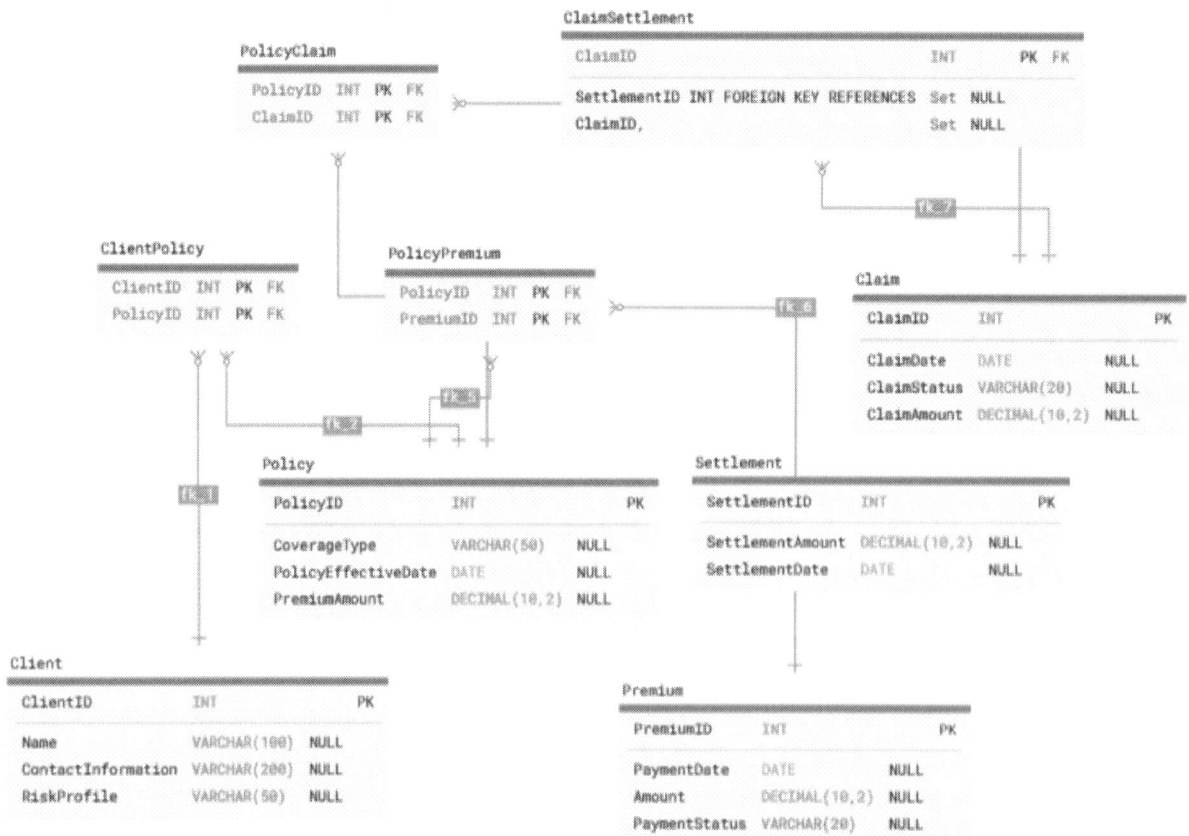

DDL for Insurance Provider Data Model for Claims Processing

```sql
-- Create the database
CREATE DATABASE InsuranceDB;
GO

USE InsuranceDB;

-- Create the Client table
CREATE TABLE Client (
    ClientID INT PRIMARY KEY,
    Name VARCHAR(100),
    ContactInformation VARCHAR(200),
    RiskProfile VARCHAR(50)
);

-- Create the Policy table
CREATE TABLE Policy (
    PolicyID INT PRIMARY KEY,
    CoverageType VARCHAR(50),
    PolicyEffectiveDate DATE,
    PremiumAmount DECIMAL(10,2)
);

-- Create the Client-Policy bridge table
CREATE TABLE ClientPolicy (
    ClientID INT FOREIGN KEY REFERENCES Client(ClientID),
    PolicyID INT FOREIGN KEY REFERENCES Policy(PolicyID),
    PRIMARY KEY (ClientID, PolicyID)
);
```

```
-- Create the Claim table
CREATE TABLE Claim (
    ClaimID INT PRIMARY KEY,
    ClaimDate DATE,
    ClaimStatus VARCHAR(20),
    ClaimAmount DECIMAL(10,2)
);


-- Create the Policy-Claim bridge table
CREATE TABLE PolicyClaim (
    PolicyID INT FOREIGN KEY REFERENCES Policy(PolicyID),
    ClaimID INT FOREIGN KEY REFERENCES Claim(ClaimID),
    PRIMARY KEY (PolicyID, ClaimID)
);


-- Create the Premium table
CREATE TABLE Premium (
    PremiumID INT PRIMARY KEY,
    PaymentDate DATE,
    Amount DECIMAL(10,2),
    PaymentStatus VARCHAR(20)
);


-- Create the Policy-Premium bridge table
CREATE TABLE PolicyPremium (
    PolicyID INT FOREIGN KEY REFERENCES Policy(PolicyID),
    PremiumID INT FOREIGN KEY REFERENCES Premium(PremiumID),
    PRIMARY KEY (PolicyID, PremiumID)
);
```

```
-- Create the Settlement table

CREATE TABLE Settlement (

    SettlementID INT PRIMARY KEY,

    SettlementAmount DECIMAL(10,2),

    SettlementDate DATE

);



-- Create the Claim-Settlement bridge table

CREATE TABLE ClaimSettlement (

    ClaimID INT FOREIGN KEY REFERENCES Claim(ClaimID),

    SettlementID INT FOREIGN KEY REFERENCES Settlement(SettlementID),

    PRIMARY KEY (ClaimID, SettlementID)

);
```

Exercise: Primary Key Selection and Relationship Derivation

Objective: Develop a data model for insurance claims, focusing on primary key selection and relationship derivation.

1. **Identify entities**: Begin with core entities, including Client, Policy, Claim, and Premium.

2. **Define primary keys**: Assign unique identifiers such as ClientID, PolicyID, ClaimID, and PremiumID.

3. **Derive relationships**: Use the following relationships to connect entities:

   - **Client - Policy**: 1:M, where each client has multiple policies.

   - **Policy - Claim**: 1:M, where each policy can have multiple claims.

   - **Policy - Premium**: 1:M, where each policy requires multiple premium payments.

4. **Diagram the model**: Using Lucidchart or ERwin, create a visual representation of these relationships, ensuring cardinality is accurately represented.

This exercise highlights how primary keys and relationships create a foundational structure for insurance data models.

Case Study: Insurance Provider Data Model for Claims Processing

This case study examines a data model designed to streamline claims processing for an insurance provider. By organizing data into relevant entities and establishing relationships, the insurer can efficiently track policies, claims, and client details.

1. **Client Information**: Client data is managed in the Client entity, storing essential information such as contact details and risk assessments.

2. **Policy Management**: The Policy entity captures details about each insurance policy, including policy type, coverage limits, and associated premiums. Each policy record links to the client who owns it.

3. **Claims Processing**: The Claim entity represents insurance claims, with attributes for claim date, status, amount, and associated policy ID. Each claim is tied to a policy record, enabling the insurance provider to track claims for each policy.

4. **Premium Collection**: Premium payments are tracked within the Premium entity, linked to specific policies. This relationship allows insurers to ensure that policies remain active based on payment status.

With this model, insurers can gain a comprehensive view of their operations, facilitating better decision-making, claims processing, and client management.

Chapter Summary and Quiz

In this chapter, we explored the following:

- The unique data needs and regulatory considerations of the insurance industry.

- Core entities within insurance data models, including Policies, Clients, Claims, and Premiums.

- How to build a conceptual data model and organize data into subject areas like Client Management, Policy Administration, and Claims Processing.

- Key relationships and cardinality in insurance models, including client-policy and policy-claim connections.

- Practical exercise in defining primary keys and relationships.

- A case study on an insurance provider's claims processing model.

Quiz:

1. What are some of the primary regulatory concerns in insurance data modeling?

2. Identify the core entities in an insurance data model and their primary attributes.

3. Describe the relationship and cardinality between Clients and Policies.

4. How can organizing data into subject areas benefit an insurance data model?

5. In the context of claims processing, how are claims and settlements typically related?

This concludes Chapter 5. With a solid understanding of insurance data modeling, we'll be ready to delve into other specialized industries in the following chapters, continuing to build on these principles and best practices.

Chapter 6: Data Modeling for the Communication Industry

Industry Overview: Structure, Key Data Elements, and Compliance

The communication industry encompasses a wide range of services, from internet and telecommunication providers to media and broadcasting companies. Data in this industry is expansive and complex, as it involves managing vast amounts of information about customers, services, network resources, and billing. Communication companies must ensure data privacy and security due to strict regulatory requirements, including standards like the General Data Protection Regulation (GDPR) and, in the United States, the Communications Assistance for Law Enforcement Act (CALEA).

This chapter explores how data models can be structured to support the communication industry's unique requirements, focusing on managing customer relationships, tracking services, and supporting network infrastructure.

Identifying Core Entities: Customers, Services, Billing, Network Resources

To structure a robust data model for communication data, we first identify and define the key entities and their attributes. Each entity encapsulates essential information that supports business functions.

1. **Customers**
   Represents individuals or organizations subscribing to one or more communication services.

   o **CustomerID** (Primary Key): Unique identifier for each customer.

   o **FirstName**: Customer's first name.

   o **LastName**: Customer's last name.

   o **DateOfBirth**: Customer's date of birth.

   o **PhoneNumber**: Primary contact number.

   o **EmailAddress**: Contact email address.

   o **BillingAddress**: Address for billing purposes.

   o **SubscriptionStatus**: Status of the customer's account (e.g., Active, Suspended).

   o **RegistrationDate**: Date of initial account creation.

2. **Services**
Describes various offerings provided to customers, such as mobile plans, internet packages, or media subscriptions.

- **ServiceID** (Primary Key): Unique identifier for each service.
- **ServiceName**: Name of the service (e.g., "Mobile Plan A").
- **Description**: Brief description of the service features.
- **ServiceType**: Type of service (e.g., Mobile, Internet, TV).
- **MonthlyCost**: Monthly subscription fee.
- **ActivationDate**: Date the service was activated.
- **ServiceStatus**: Current status (e.g., Active, Inactive).
- **NetworkResourceID** (Foreign Key): References network resources required for service delivery.

3. **Billing**
Captures details of billing information associated with each customer and their subscribed services.

- **BillingID** (Primary Key): Unique identifier for each billing record.
- **CustomerID** (Foreign Key): Links to the customer being billed.
- **BillingDate**: Date of the billing cycle.
- **DueDate**: Due date for payment.
- **AmountDue**: Total amount to be paid.
- **PaidAmount**: Amount that has been paid by the customer.
- **BillingStatus**: Status of payment (e.g., Paid, Unpaid, Overdue).
- **ServiceID** (Foreign Key): References the service billed.

4. **Network Resources**
Represents the physical or virtual infrastructure elements that support various services.

- **ResourceID** (Primary Key): Unique identifier for each network resource.
- **ResourceName**: Name of the resource (e.g., Tower123).
- **ResourceType**: Type of network component (e.g., Router, Cell Tower).
- **Location**: Physical location of the resource.
- **Status**: Operational status (e.g., Active, Maintenance).
- **Capacity**: Resource capacity or bandwidth available.

o **AssignedServiceID** (Foreign Key): Links to the services that utilize this network resource.

Creating a Conceptual Model for Communication

In building a conceptual model, we begin by defining high-level entities and their relationships without delving into specific attributes or database schema requirements. This model provides a simplified view of the structure of the communication data, outlining core entities and their interactions.

For example, a conceptual model might show:

- **Customer-Services Relationship**: A customer may subscribe to multiple services, creating a one-to-many (1:M) relationship.

- **Services-Network Resources Relationship**: Each service depends on one or more network resources, establishing a many-to-many (M:M) relationship.

- **Customer-Billing Relationship**: A customer can have multiple bills, indicating a 1:M relationship between Customer and Billing.

This conceptual view offers a roadmap for more detailed modeling and guides the creation of subject areas in the next steps.

Subject Areas: Customer Management, Network Services, Billing

To manage the complexity of communication data, we divide the model into key subject areas. Each subject area addresses a different aspect of the industry's data needs.

1. **Customer Management**: Contains all data related to customer identities, including profiles, contact information, service subscriptions, and billing history. This subject area is crucial for managing customer interactions and service personalization.

2. **Network Services**: Covers data on available services, network components, and infrastructure dependencies. This area also includes the assignment of network resources to specific services and customers.

3. **Billing**: Focuses on invoices, payments, and financial transactions associated with customers and services. The billing subject area captures payment history, outstanding balances, and billing cycles.

Breaking the model into these subject areas allows us to maintain clarity and ensure that each aspect of the data aligns with the industry's business requirements.

Cardinality and Relationship Analysis in Communication Models

Cardinality in the communication industry model defines the nature of relationships between entities, which can be complex given the wide variety of interactions among customers, services, and network resources. Key relationships include:

- **Customer to Service**: A single customer can subscribe to multiple services, such as internet, mobile, and TV packages, creating a 1:M relationship.

- **Service to Network Resources**: Each service may rely on multiple network components, while network resources are shared across services, forming an M:M relationship.

- **Customer to Billing**: For each billing period, a customer may have one invoice, and each invoice is unique to a customer, supporting a 1:M relationship.

Analyzing these relationships helps us model the industry's data flows and accurately reflects how entities interact with each other.

Logical Model for Telecom Service Provider

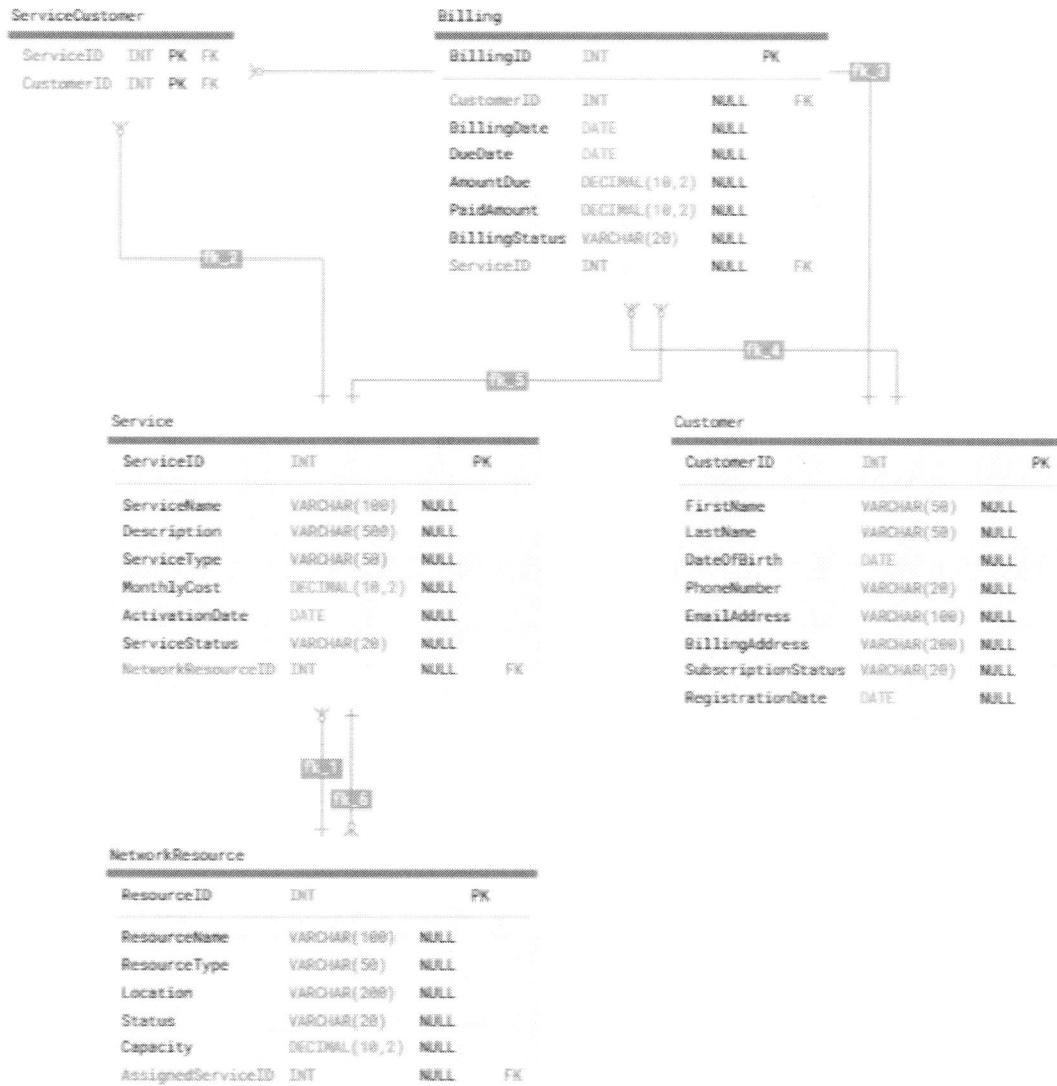

DDL for Telecom Service Provider

-- Create the database

CREATE DATABASE CommunicationDB;

GO

USE CommunicationDB;

-- Create the Customer table

CREATE TABLE Customer (

    CustomerID INT PRIMARY KEY,

    FirstName VARCHAR(50),

    LastName VARCHAR(50),

    DateOfBirth DATE,

    PhoneNumber VARCHAR(20),

    EmailAddress VARCHAR(100),

    BillingAddress VARCHAR(200),

    SubscriptionStatus VARCHAR(20),

    RegistrationDate DATE

);

-- Create the Service table

CREATE TABLE Service (

    ServiceID INT PRIMARY KEY,

    ServiceName VARCHAR(100),

    [Description] VARCHAR(500),

    ServiceType VARCHAR(50),

    MonthlyCost DECIMAL(10,2),

    ActivationDate DATE,

    ServiceStatus VARCHAR(20),

    NetworkResourceID INT FOREIGN KEY REFERENCES NetworkResource(ResourceID)

);

-- Create the Service-Customer bridge table

CREATE TABLE ServiceCustomer (

    ServiceID INT FOREIGN KEY REFERENCES Service(ServiceID),

Michael E. Kirshteyn, Ph.D

```
    CustomerID INT FOREIGN KEY REFERENCES Customer(CustomerID),

    PRIMARY KEY (ServiceID, CustomerID)

);


-- Create the Billing table

CREATE TABLE Billing (

    BillingID INT PRIMARY KEY,

    CustomerID INT FOREIGN KEY REFERENCES Customer(CustomerID),

    BillingDate DATE,

    DueDate DATE,

    AmountDue DECIMAL(10,2),

    PaidAmount DECIMAL(10,2),

    BillingStatus VARCHAR(20),

    ServiceID INT FOREIGN KEY REFERENCES Service(ServiceID)

);


-- Create the NetworkResource table

CREATE TABLE NetworkResource (

    ResourceID INT PRIMARY KEY,

    ResourceName VARCHAR(100),

    ResourceType VARCHAR(50),

    [Location] VARCHAR(200),

    [Status] VARCHAR(20),

    Capacity DECIMAL(10,2),

    AssignedServiceID INT FOREIGN KEY REFERENCES Service(ServiceID)

);
```

Exercise: Service-Customer and Billing Relationships

In this exercise, you'll practice modeling relationships by defining a data model that captures customer service subscriptions and billing cycles.

Steps:

1. **Identify Primary Keys**: Define unique identifiers for Customers, Services, and Billing entities.

2. **Define Foreign Keys**: Establish foreign keys for Customer-Service relationships and Customer-Billing relationships.

3. **Determine Relationship Type**: Specify the cardinality for each relationship.

4. **Create the Model**: Diagram the Customer, Service, and Billing entities, showing primary keys, foreign keys, and cardinality.

This exercise will enhance your ability to map out relationships and understand the dependencies among entities in the communication model.

Case Study: Data Model for Telecom Service Provider

Consider a telecom provider offering mobile, internet, and TV services. The provider needs a data model that links customers to services, tracks the status of network resources, and manages billing information.

1. **Customer Management**: Customer profiles are connected to their subscribed services and billing records. Each customer can have multiple service subscriptions, which are managed within a customer management system.

2. **Network Services and Resources**: Each service has specific resource requirements, such as bandwidth for internet services or broadcast channels for TV. Network resources are allocated to services based on customer demand, and monitoring these allocations ensures efficient service delivery.

3. **Billing and Payment**: Billing records are generated for each customer based on their subscribed services and usage. The model must support monthly billing cycles, detailed usage records, and automated payment processing.

This case study provides a real-world example of how data models support complex interactions in the communication industry.

Chapter Summary and Quiz

In this chapter, we explored data modeling for the communication industry. We covered key industry entities like customers, services, billing, and network resources, examined cardinality in entity relationships, and worked through exercises and a case study to build a comprehensive model for a telecom provider.

Quiz:

1. List the core entities typically included in a communication industry data model.

2. Explain the purpose of network resources in the communication industry.

3. Describe the cardinality between Customer and Billing entities.

4. In a telecom provider model, how would you model a many-to-many relationship between Services and Network Resources?

By completing this chapter, you have gained insights into the complexities of data modeling in the communication industry, preparing you to address unique challenges related to customer management, network services, and billing.

Chapter 7: Data Modeling for Blockchain-Based Applications

Introduction to Blockchain and Distributed Ledger Technology

Blockchain technology, also known as Distributed Ledger Technology (DLT), provides a decentralized and secure way to record transactions across a distributed network. Rather than relying on a central authority, blockchain applications use cryptographic protocols to ensure data integrity, transparency, and trust. Each participant in a blockchain network has a copy of the ledger, and once recorded, data on a blockchain is immutable, making it ideal for applications requiring high security and tamper-resistant record-keeping.

This chapter focuses on data modeling essentials for blockchain-based applications, identifying core components and establishing relationships that support the decentralized nature of blockchain data.

Key Blockchain Components: Transactions, Blocks, Nodes, Participants

To effectively structure data for blockchain applications, we must identify and define key components that form the blockchain's backbone.

1. Transactions

Represents individual actions recorded on the blockchain, such as asset transfers or contract executions.

- **TransactionID** (Primary Key): Unique identifier for each transaction.

- **Timestamp**: Date and time when the transaction is created.

- **Amount**: Quantity or value involved in the transaction (e.g., tokens, currency).

- **SenderID** (Foreign Key): Links to the participant initiating the transaction.

- **ReceiverID** (Foreign Key): Links to the participant receiving the asset or data.

- **TransactionType**: Type of transaction (e.g., transfer, contract, verification).

- **Status**: Current status (e.g., Pending, Completed, Rejected).

- **BlockID** (Foreign Key): Links to the block containing this transaction.

2. Blocks

A block contains a batch of transactions and serves as the foundational unit for storing data on a blockchain.

- **BlockID** (Primary Key): Unique identifier for each block.

- **PreviousBlockID**: Links to the preceding block in the chain.

- **Timestamp**: Date and time when the block was created.

- **Nonce**: Random number used to meet the blockchain's difficulty level.

- **MerkleRoot**: Cryptographic hash representing all transactions within the block.

- **TransactionCount**: Number of transactions in the block.

3. Nodes

Represents the devices or servers participating in the blockchain network, maintaining copies of the ledger, validating transactions, and creating new blocks.

- **NodeID** (Primary Key): Unique identifier for each node.

- **NodeAddress**: Network address of the node.

- **Role**: Role of the node in the network (e.g., Miner, Validator, Observer).

- **Status**: Current status (e.g., Active, Inactive).

- **LastActiveDate**: Last recorded activity date.

4. Participants

Blockchain participants are individuals, organizations, or systems that initiate transactions, validate records, or observe the network.

- **ParticipantID** (Primary Key): Unique identifier for each participant.

- **Name**: Name of the individual or organization.

- **Role**: Role in the blockchain network (e.g., Sender, Receiver, Validator).

- **PublicKey**: Unique cryptographic key associated with the participant.

- **WalletAddress**: Address linked to the participant's digital wallet.

Building a Conceptual Model for Blockchain

A conceptual model for blockchain highlights the primary components and their relationships. Blockchain networks are based on interconnected nodes and blocks that manage transactions across the network. Key relationships include:

- **Participant-Transaction Relationship**: Each transaction involves two participants (sender and receiver), creating a self-referential one-to-many (1:M) relationship within the Participants entity.

- **Transaction-Block Relationship**: Each block may contain multiple transactions, forming a one-to-many (1:M) relationship between Block and Transaction.

- **Block-Blockchain Relationship**: Blocks are sequentially linked, with each block referencing the previous one, creating a one-to-one (1:1) relationship within the Blocks entity.

This conceptual model helps in structuring data within a decentralized ledger system.

Subject Area Breakdown: Ledger, Network Participants, Transaction Records

Dividing the blockchain data model into subject areas allows us to address the specific functions and structures unique to blockchain applications.

1. Ledger

The ledger represents the entire blockchain sequence, where each block contains a set of transactions. This subject area focuses on the block chain's structure, from genesis to the latest block.

- **Entities**: Blocks, Transactions.
- **Primary Relationships**: Block to Transaction (1:M), Block to Block (1:1 for linking sequential blocks).

2. Network Participants

This subject area covers participants within the blockchain, including senders, receivers, and validators. It stores participant information and cryptographic keys, enabling secure and authenticated transactions.

- **Entities**: Participants, Transactions.

- **Primary Relationships**: Participant to Transaction (1:M), Transaction to Participant (1:M through SenderID and ReceiverID).

3. Transaction Records

Transaction records log each individual transaction, including participants, time stamps, and amounts. It includes detailed information essential for transaction integrity.

- **Entities**: Transactions, Blocks.

- **Primary Relationships**: Transaction to Block (1:M).

Relationship Derivation and Cardinality in Blockchain Models

Blockchain data models are unique because they must capture the immutability, transparency, and security of transactions.

- **Participant to Transaction**: Each participant may initiate multiple transactions over time, forming a one-to-many (1:M) relationship between Participant and Transaction.

- **Transaction to Block**: Each block contains multiple transactions, making this a one-to-many (1:M) relationship.

- **Block to Block**: Blocks are sequentially linked, with each block referencing the previous one, resulting in a one-to-one (1:1) relationship to preserve chain integrity.

The cardinality in blockchain ensures all transactions and blocks are traceable, reliable, and immutable.

Logical Model for Blockchain-Based Applications

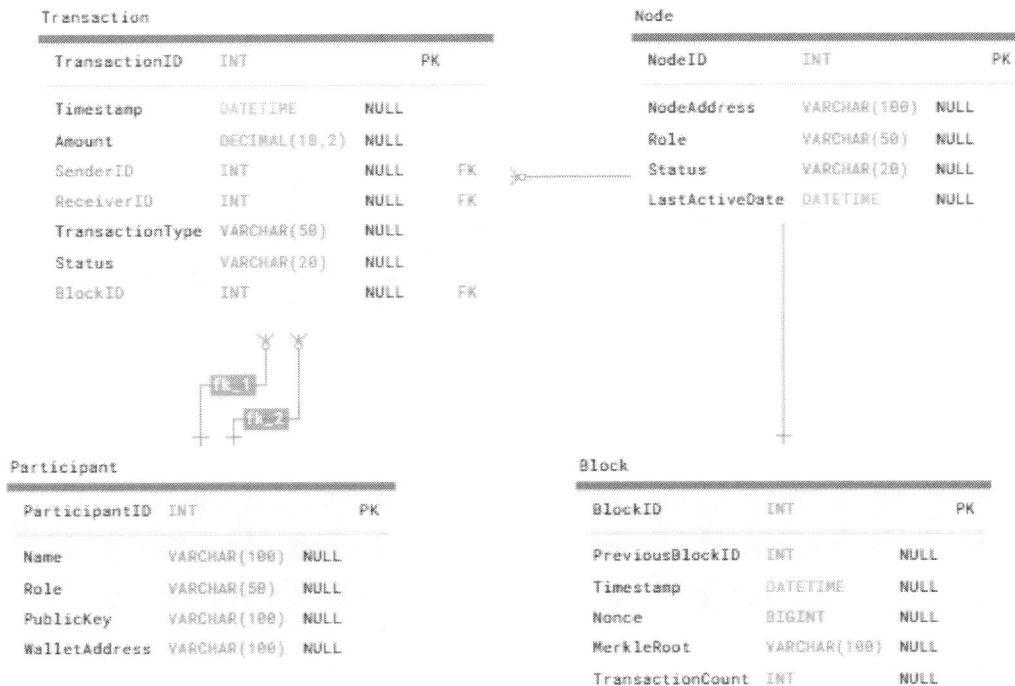

Transaction

TransactionID	INT		PK
Timestamp	DATETIME	NULL	
Amount	DECIMAL(18,2)	NULL	
SenderID	INT	NULL	FK
ReceiverID	INT	NULL	FK
TransactionType	VARCHAR(50)	NULL	
Status	VARCHAR(20)	NULL	
BlockID	INT	NULL	FK

Node

NodeID	INT		PK
NodeAddress	VARCHAR(100)	NULL	
Role	VARCHAR(50)	NULL	
Status	VARCHAR(20)	NULL	
LastActiveDate	DATETIME	NULL	

Participant

ParticipantID	INT		PK
Name	VARCHAR(100)	NULL	
Role	VARCHAR(50)	NULL	
PublicKey	VARCHAR(100)	NULL	
WalletAddress	VARCHAR(100)	NULL	

Block

BlockID	INT		PK
PreviousBlockID	INT	NULL	
Timestamp	DATETIME	NULL	
Nonce	BIGINT	NULL	
MerkleRoot	VARCHAR(100)	NULL	
TransactionCount	INT	NULL	

DDL for Blockchain Models

-- Create the database

CREATE DATABASE BlockchainDB;

GO

USE BlockchainDB;

-- Create the Participant table

CREATE TABLE Participant (

   ParticipantID INT PRIMARY KEY,

   [Name] VARCHAR(100),

   [Role] VARCHAR(50),

```
    PublicKey VARCHAR(100),

    WalletAddress VARCHAR(100)
);


-- Create the Transaction table
CREATE TABLE [Transaction] (

    TransactionID INT PRIMARY KEY,

    [Timestamp] DATETIME,

    [Amount] DECIMAL(18,2),

    SenderID INT FOREIGN KEY REFERENCES Participant(ParticipantID),

    ReceiverID INT FOREIGN KEY REFERENCES Participant(ParticipantID),

    [TransactionType] VARCHAR(50),

    [Status] VARCHAR(20),

    BlockID INT FOREIGN KEY REFERENCES [Block](BlockID)
);


-- Create the Block table
CREATE TABLE [Block] (

    BlockID INT PRIMARY KEY,

    PreviousBlockID INT,

    [Timestamp] DATETIME,

    [Nonce] BIGINT,

    MerkleRoot VARCHAR(100),

    TransactionCount INT
);


-- Create the Node table
CREATE TABLE [Node] (

    NodeID INT PRIMARY KEY,

    NodeAddress VARCHAR(100),
```

```
    [Role] VARCHAR(50),

    [Status] VARCHAR(20),

    LastActiveDate DATETIME

);
```

Exercise: Modeling Transactions and Ledger Relationships

In this exercise, you'll design the relationships between participants, transactions, and blocks.

Steps:

1. **Identify Primary Keys and Foreign Keys**: Define unique identifiers and foreign keys for each entity.

2. **Determine Relationship Type**: Specify the cardinality for each relationship.

3. **Diagram the Model**: Map out Participants, Transactions, and Blocks with attributes, primary keys, and foreign keys.

Completing this exercise reinforces the importance of designing a decentralized ledger that maintains integrity, transparency, and security.

Case Study: Blockchain Data Model for Asset Management

Consider a blockchain-based asset management system that records asset transfers. The data model needs to track participants (asset holders), transactions (asset transfers), and blocks (record containers).

1. Ledger Structure

A blockchain ledger records blocks sequentially, each holding multiple asset transfers. This structure supports secure, transparent record-keeping, ensuring asset transfer data is reliable and traceable.

2. **Participants and Transactions**

Each participant has a unique public key, securely identified during asset transfers. Transactions record transfer details, from sender and receiver to transaction amount.

3. **Block Linkage**

Each block links to its predecessor, ensuring the integrity of the blockchain. This linkage secures the entire chain by requiring data consistency across all records.

This case study demonstrates how blockchain data models facilitate secure asset management across a decentralized network.

Chapter Summary and Quiz

In this chapter, we examined data modeling for blockchain-based applications, identifying core entities, attributes, and relationships. We developed a conceptual model, practiced relationship derivation, and explored asset management in a blockchain setting.

Quiz:

1. List key entities and their attributes in a blockchain data model.

2. Describe the cardinality between Participants and Transactions.

3. Explain how blockchain ensures data immutability and security.

4. What is the purpose of linking blocks in a blockchain?

By understanding blockchain data models, you're equipped to design secure and efficient systems for recording transactions and managing assets in a decentralized environment.

Chapter 8: Data Modeling for the Internet of Things (IoT)

Overview of IoT Data Structure and Components

The Internet of Things (IoT) represents a vast network of connected devices and sensors that communicate and exchange data across various environments. From smart homes to industrial systems, IoT enables automation, real-time monitoring, and improved decision-making. Data modeling for IoT systems must accommodate large volumes of streaming data, diverse device types, and complex interactions among entities.

This chapter explores the essential components of IoT data modeling, focusing on the relationships between devices, sensors, users, and data streams. We'll build a conceptual model tailored to IoT and analyze the cardinality that reflects real-world data flow.

Key IoT Entities: Devices, Sensors, Data Streams, Users

IoT data models must represent the core entities involved in data generation, transfer, and usage. Below are the primary entities in an IoT data model, along with their key attributes:

1. **Devices**

   Represents the connected objects in an IoT ecosystem, such as thermostats, cameras, and wearable tech.

   - **DeviceID** (Primary Key): Unique identifier for each device.

   - **DeviceType**: Type or category of the device (e.g., thermostat, camera).

   - **Manufacturer**: Company that manufactured the device.

   - **Model**: Model number or name.

   - **FirmwareVersion**: Firmware version currently installed.

   - **Status**: Current status of the device (e.g., Active, Inactive).

   - **LocationID** (Foreign Key): Links to the location entity where the device is installed.

2. Sensors

Physical components embedded in devices that measure and report specific data points, such as temperature or humidity.

- **SensorID** (Primary Key): Unique identifier for each sensor.

- **SensorType**: Type of sensor (e.g., temperature, humidity, motion).

- **MeasurementUnit**: Unit of measurement (e.g., Celsius, percentage).

- **DeviceID** (Foreign Key): Links to the device entity that the sensor belongs to.

- **Status**: Indicates if the sensor is operational or offline.

- **CalibrationDate**: Last calibration date to ensure data accuracy.

3. Data Streams

Represents the continuous flow of data generated by sensors over time.

- **StreamID** (Primary Key): Unique identifier for each data stream.

- **SensorID** (Foreign Key): Links to the sensor generating the data stream.

- **Timestamp**: Date and time of the data capture.

- **DataValue**: The recorded value from the sensor.

- **QualityFlag**: Indicator of data quality (e.g., Normal, Low).

- **Frequency**: Frequency of data reporting (e.g., every 10 seconds).

4. Users

Represents individuals or systems interacting with IoT devices and data, such as residents in a smart home or operators in an industrial setting.

- **UserID** (Primary Key): Unique identifier for each user.

- **Username**: Name or alias used by the user.

- **Role**: Role in the IoT system (e.g., Admin, Viewer).

- **AccessLevel**: Permissions associated with the user's role.

- **DeviceID** (Foreign Key): Links to specific devices the user has access to.

Constructing the Conceptual Model for IoT

The IoT conceptual model represents the interconnections between devices, sensors, data streams, and users. The core relationships include:

- **Device-Sensor Relationship**: Each device can have multiple sensors, creating a one-to-many (1:M) relationship.

- **Sensor-Data Stream Relationship**: Each sensor can generate multiple data streams over time, establishing another one-to-many (1:M) relationship.

- **User-Device Relationship**: Each user can access multiple devices, creating a many-to-many (M:N) relationship, which we resolve with an associative table.

By structuring these entities and relationships, the IoT conceptual model supports robust data management and interaction within an IoT network.

Subject Areas: Device Management, Data Collection, User Interaction

1. Device Management

This subject area manages devices' lifecycle, including registration, configuration, firmware updates, and status monitoring.

- **Entities**: Devices, Sensors.
- **Primary Relationships**: Device to Sensor (1:M).
- **Attributes**: Device type, status, location, sensor calibration, and operational details.

2. Data Collection

Centralizes the capture and storage of data generated by sensors, essential for analysis and reporting in IoT applications.

- **Entities**: Sensors, Data Streams.

- **Primary Relationships**: Sensor to Data Stream (1:M).

- **Attributes**: Data timestamp, value, quality, frequency.

3. User Interaction

Supports user access and permissions, allowing users to interact with and control devices in the IoT ecosystem.

- **Entities**: Users, Devices.

- **Primary Relationships**: User to Device (M:N).

- **Attributes**: User role, access levels, device assignment.

Analyzing Relationships and Cardinality in IoT Models

IoT data models need to represent the complex relationships between devices, sensors, and data streams accurately.

- **Device-Sensor Relationship**: Each device typically contains multiple sensors for different measurements (e.g., temperature, humidity), forming a one-to-many (1:M) relationship.

- **Sensor-Data Stream Relationship**: Each sensor generates multiple data records over time, creating a one-to-many (1:M) relationship.

- **User-Device Relationship**: Users can control or monitor multiple devices, and each device may have multiple users with varying access levels, making it a many-to-many (M:N) relationship.

By modeling these relationships, we ensure data integrity and create a structure capable of handling complex IoT interactions.

IoT Logical Model

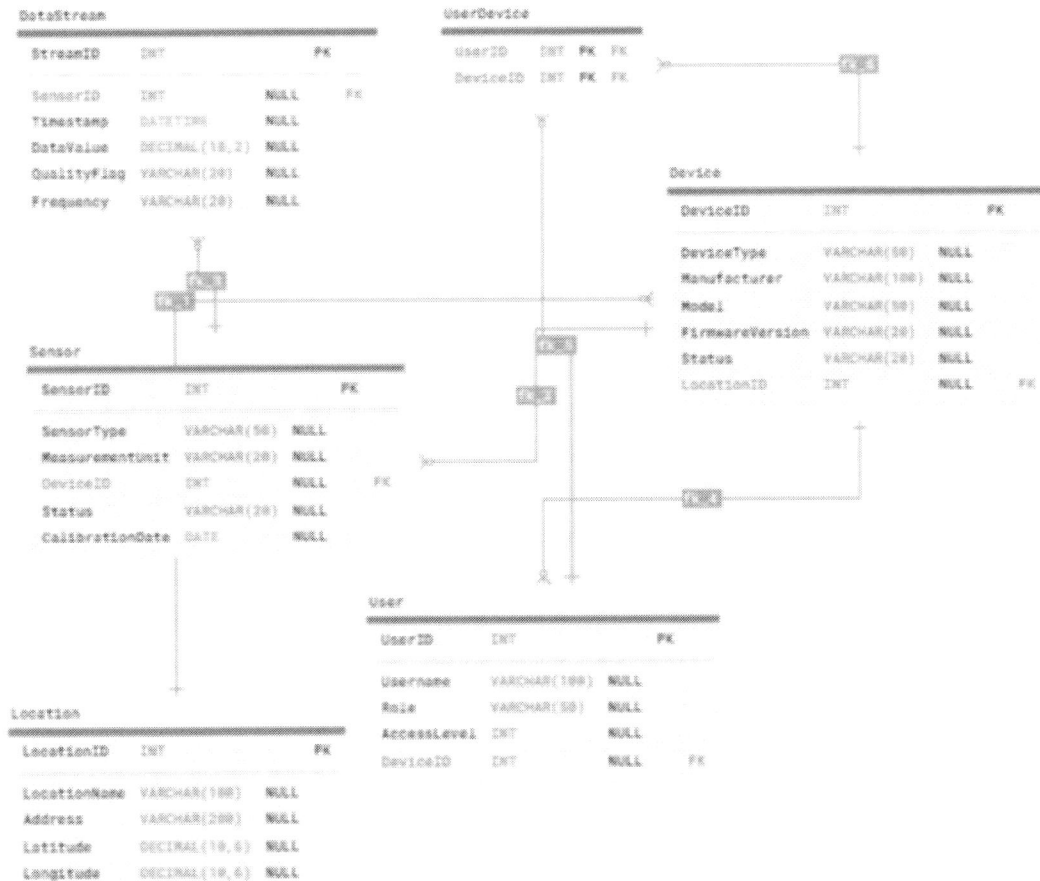

DDL for IoT

-- Create the database

CREATE DATABASE IoTDB;

GO

USE IoTDB;

-- Create the Device table

CREATE TABLE Device (

    DeviceID INT PRIMARY KEY,

```
    DeviceType VARCHAR(50),

    Manufacturer VARCHAR(100),

    Model VARCHAR(50),

    FirmwareVersion VARCHAR(20),

    [Status] VARCHAR(20),

    LocationID INT FOREIGN KEY REFERENCES Location(LocationID)
);


-- Create the Sensor table
CREATE TABLE Sensor (

    SensorID INT PRIMARY KEY,

    SensorType VARCHAR(50),

    MeasurementUnit VARCHAR(20),

    DeviceID INT FOREIGN KEY REFERENCES Device(DeviceID),

    [Status] VARCHAR(20),

    CalibrationDate DATE
);


-- Create the DataStream table
CREATE TABLE DataStream (

    StreamID INT PRIMARY KEY,

    SensorID INT FOREIGN KEY REFERENCES Sensor(SensorID),

    [Timestamp] DATETIME,

    DataValue DECIMAL(18,2),

    QualityFlag VARCHAR(20),

    [Frequency] VARCHAR(20)
);


-- Create the User table
CREATE TABLE [User] (
```

```
    UserID INT PRIMARY KEY,

    Username VARCHAR(100),

    [Role] VARCHAR(50),

    AccessLevel INT,

    DeviceID INT FOREIGN KEY REFERENCES Device(DeviceID)

);


-- Create the User-Device bridge table

CREATE TABLE UserDevice (

    UserID INT FOREIGN KEY REFERENCES [User](UserID),

    DeviceID INT FOREIGN KEY REFERENCES Device(DeviceID),

    PRIMARY KEY (UserID, DeviceID)

);


-- Create the Location table

CREATE TABLE Location (

    LocationID INT PRIMARY KEY,

    LocationName VARCHAR(100),

    Address VARCHAR(200),

    Latitude DECIMAL(10,6),

    Longitude DECIMAL(10,6)

);
```

Exercise: Modeling Sensor-Device and Data Relationships

In this exercise, you will create a basic data model illustrating relationships between sensors, devices, and data streams in an IoT network.

Steps:

1. **Define Keys and Attributes**: Identify primary and foreign keys for each entity, and list their attributes.

2. **Map Relationships**: Determine cardinality for each relationship (e.g., Device-Sensor, Sensor-Data Stream).

3. **Create Diagram**: Sketch out the entities and relationships with primary and foreign key connections.

This exercise reinforces understanding of data structure within an IoT ecosystem, preparing you for real-world applications.

Case Study: IoT Data Model for Smart Home Application

A smart home system allows residents to control devices like thermostats, security cameras, and lighting from an app. The data model for this application focuses on managing devices, capturing data, and supporting user interactions.

1. Device Management

The model includes entities for managing devices in various rooms, each with multiple sensors tracking temperature, humidity, and motion.

2. Data Collection and Analysis

Each sensor records data at regular intervals, creating continuous data streams. These records are essential for detecting patterns and automating responses (e.g., adjusting temperature).

3. User Access and Control

Users with varying access levels (e.g., homeowners, guests) can control specific devices. Role-based access ensures only authorized users can change device settings.

This case study demonstrates how data models in IoT applications enable automation, monitoring, and user control in a smart environment.

Chapter Summary and Quiz

In this chapter, we explored IoT data modeling, identifying key entities and relationships necessary for capturing complex IoT data interactions. Through exercises and case studies, we built foundational knowledge of IoT structures, from devices to data streams.

Quiz:

1. List the primary entities in an IoT data model.

2. Describe the relationship between Devices and Sensors.

3. How is user access modeled in IoT applications?

4. Explain the importance of data streams in IoT.

By understanding IoT data models, you are prepared to design data structures that can handle large-scale, real-time data and support complex interactions between devices and users in connected systems.

Chapter 9: Data Modeling for the Finance and Banking Industry

Overview of Finance and Banking Data Needs and Regulatory Requirements

The finance and banking sector is data-intensive, requiring precise and secure data management. Financial institutions manage a variety of data types, from customer details and account information to transactional records and loan details. These systems must adhere to stringent regulatory requirements, including anti-money laundering (AML) and Know Your Customer (KYC) standards, as well as data privacy laws like GDPR and CCPA. Financial data models must prioritize data integrity, privacy, and security while enabling complex transactions, detailed reporting, and analytics.

This chapter covers essential components and entities involved in finance data modeling, focusing on critical relationships and subject areas essential for banking applications.

Key Entities: Accounts, Transactions, Customers, Loans, Interest Rates

Finance data models focus on core entities central to banking operations. Below are the primary entities in a banking data model, along with their key attributes:

1. **Accounts**

   Represents financial accounts held by customers, such as checking, savings, and investment accounts.

   - **AccountID** (Primary Key): Unique identifier for each account.
   - **AccountType**: Type of account (e.g., Checking, Savings, Loan).
   - **Balance**: Current balance in the account.
   - **OpenDate**: Date the account was opened.
   - **Status**: Current status (e.g., Active, Closed).
   - **CustomerID** (Foreign Key): Links to the customer who owns the account.

2. **Transactions**

Represents the movement of funds in and out of accounts, including deposits, withdrawals, and transfers.

- **TransactionID** (Primary Key): Unique identifier for each transaction.

- **AccountID** (Foreign Key): Links to the account associated with the transaction.

- **TransactionType**: Type of transaction (e.g., Deposit, Withdrawal, Transfer).

- **Amount**: Amount of the transaction.

- **TransactionDate**: Date and time of the transaction.

- **Description**: Description or memo for the transaction.

3. Customers

Represents individuals or entities holding accounts and utilizing bank services.

- **CustomerID** (Primary Key): Unique identifier for each customer.

- **Name**: Full name of the customer.

- **DateOfBirth**: Customer's date of birth (for individual accounts).

- **ContactInfo**: Customer's contact information (phone, email, address).

- **SSN**: Social Security Number (or similar identifier, depending on location).

- **Status**: Customer status (e.g., Active, Suspended).

- **RiskRating**: Risk rating for AML purposes.

4. Loans

Represents financial products lent to customers, such as mortgages, personal loans, and business loans.

- **LoanID** (Primary Key): Unique identifier for each loan.

- **LoanType**: Type of loan (e.g., Mortgage, Auto Loan).

- **PrincipalAmount**: Original loan amount.

- **InterestRate**: Interest rate applied to the loan.

- **StartDate**: Date the loan originated.

- **Term**: Loan term or duration.

- **AccountID** (Foreign Key): Links to the account related to the loan.

5. Interest Rates

Represents the rates applied to various loan products, which may fluctuate over time.

- **RateID** (Primary Key): Unique identifier for each interest rate entry.

- **LoanType** (Foreign Key): Links to the type of loan the rate applies to.

- **Rate**: Interest rate percentage.

- **EffectiveDate**: Date when the interest rate became effective.

- **ExpiryDate**: Date when the interest rate expires or changes.

Constructing a Finance Conceptual Model

The finance conceptual model represents entities and relationships critical to a financial institution's operations, including accounts, transactions, and customer details. Key relationships include:

- **Customer-Account Relationship**: A customer can have multiple accounts, forming a one-to-many (1:M) relationship.

- **Account-Transaction Relationship**: Each account can be involved in multiple transactions, creating another one-to-many (1:M) relationship.

- **Account-Loan Relationship**: An account may have one or more loans associated with it, depending on loan products accessed by the customer.

This foundational model supports data integrity, allows financial analysis, and helps banks manage compliance and reporting effectively.

Subject Areas: Customer Accounts, Transactions, Loan Management, Compliance

1. Customer Accounts

This subject area focuses on managing account details, account types, balances, and ownership information.

- **Entities**: Customers, Accounts.

- **Primary Relationships**: Customer to Account (1:M).

- **Attributes**: Account type, balance, open date, status.

2. Transactions

Central to managing all financial activities, this subject area captures deposits, withdrawals, and transfers, as well as historical tracking.

- **Entities**: Accounts, Transactions.

- **Primary Relationships**: Account to Transaction (1:M).

- **Attributes**: Transaction type, amount, date, description.

3. Loan Management

Manages loan products provided to customers, including loan terms, interest rates, and payment schedules.

- **Entities**: Accounts, Loans, Interest Rates.

- **Primary Relationships**: Account to Loan (1:M).

- **Attributes**: Loan type, principal amount, interest rate, start date, term.

4. Compliance

Encompasses customer information necessary for regulatory compliance, such as KYC and AML details.

- **Entities**: Customers, Risk Ratings.

- **Primary Relationships**: Customer to Risk Rating (1:M).

- **Attributes**: Customer's risk rating, account details, contact information.

Cardinality and Complex Relationships in Finance Models

Finance data models often feature complex relationships to account for various financial interactions:

- **Customer-Account Relationship**: Each customer can have multiple accounts, reflecting a one-to-many (1:M) relationship.

- **Account-Transaction Relationship**: Accounts frequently have numerous associated transactions, creating a one-to-many (1:M) relationship.

- **Account-Loan Relationship**: An account may be linked to multiple loans, each with unique terms and interest rates, forming another one-to-many (1:M) relationship.

These cardinalities ensure accurate tracking of financial activities and adherence to compliance standards.

Logical Model for the Finance and Banking Industry

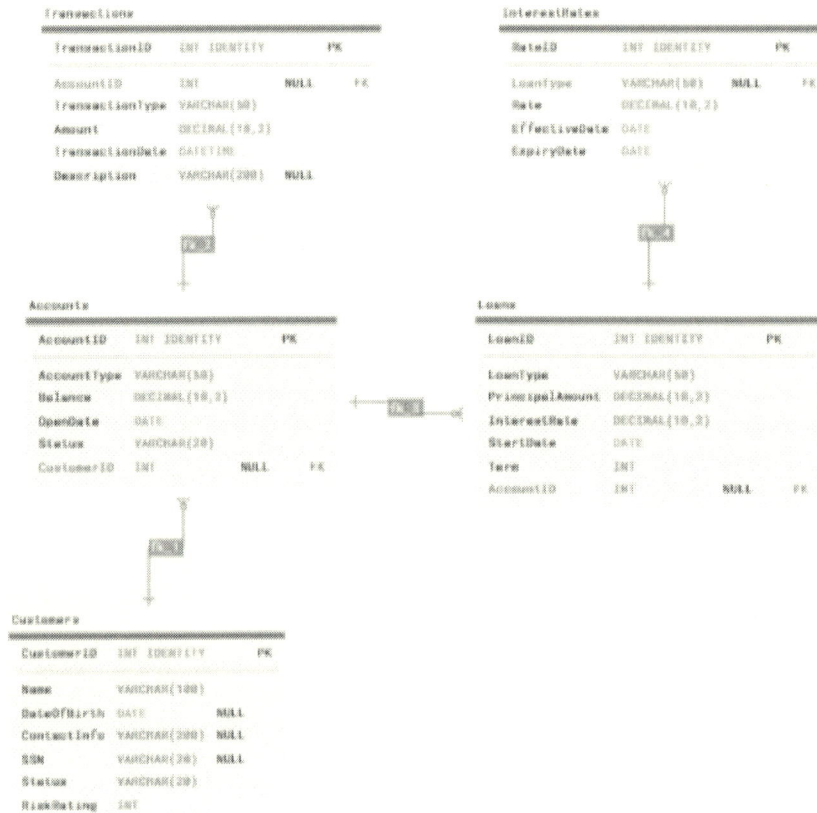

DDL for the Finance and Banking Industry

-- Customers Table

CREATE TABLE Customers (

    CustomerID INT IDENTITY(1,1) PRIMARY KEY,

    Name VARCHAR(100) NOT NULL,

    DateOfBirth DATE,

    ContactInfo VARCHAR(200),

    SSN VARCHAR(20),

    Status VARCHAR(20) NOT NULL,

```
    RiskRating INT NOT NULL
);


-- Accounts Table
CREATE TABLE Accounts (
    AccountID INT IDENTITY(1,1) PRIMARY KEY,
    AccountType VARCHAR(50) NOT NULL,
    Balance DECIMAL(18,2) NOT NULL,
    OpenDate DATE NOT NULL,
    Status VARCHAR(20) NOT NULL,
    CustomerID INT FOREIGN KEY REFERENCES Customers(CustomerID)
);


-- Transactions Table
CREATE TABLE Transactions (
    TransactionID INT IDENTITY(1,1) PRIMARY KEY,
    AccountID INT FOREIGN KEY REFERENCES Accounts(AccountID),
    TransactionType VARCHAR(50) NOT NULL,
    Amount DECIMAL(18,2) NOT NULL,
    TransactionDate DATETIME NOT NULL,
    [Description] VARCHAR(200)
);


-- Loans Table
CREATE TABLE Loans (
    LoanID INT IDENTITY(1,1) PRIMARY KEY,
    LoanType VARCHAR(50) NOT NULL,
    PrincipalAmount DECIMAL(18,2) NOT NULL,
    InterestRate DECIMAL(10,2) NOT NULL,
    StartDate DATE NOT NULL,
```

```
    [Term] INT NOT NULL,

    AccountID INT FOREIGN KEY REFERENCES Accounts(AccountID)

);


-- Interest Rates Table

CREATE TABLE InterestRates (

    RateID INT IDENTITY(1,1) PRIMARY KEY,

    LoanType VARCHAR(50) FOREIGN KEY REFERENCES Loans(LoanType),

    Rate DECIMAL(10,2) NOT NULL,

    EffectiveDate DATE NOT NULL,

    ExpiryDate DATE NOT NULL

);
```

Exercise: Modeling Transactions and Loan Relationships

In this exercise, you'll model the relationships between accounts, transactions, and loans, applying cardinalities and primary keys for consistency.

Steps:

1. **Define Keys and Attributes**: Identify primary keys for each entity, and establish foreign keys for linking related entities.

2. **Map Relationships**: Determine cardinalities for relationships between entities.

3. **Diagram Creation**: Draw a conceptual model diagram showing key entities and their relationships.

Through this exercise, you'll gain hands-on experience in structuring financial data.

Case Study: Data Model for a Banking System

Consider a banking system that manages customer accounts, processes transactions, and supports loan products. Key model features include:

1. Customer Management

Tracks customer information, including KYC details, risk assessments, and account relationships.

2. Account and Transaction Management

Represents the primary structure for handling deposits, withdrawals, and transfers. Each transaction links to an account and stores details for reporting and reconciliation.

3. Loan Tracking

Maintains loan details and repayment schedules, calculating interest and linking to customer accounts. This data supports loan risk assessment and repayment management.

This case study illustrates a practical financial data model designed to ensure compliance, efficiency, and accurate reporting in a banking environment.

Chapter Summary and Quiz

In this chapter, we discussed data modeling essentials in finance, focusing on customer, account, transaction, and loan management. We explored relationships central to banking, practiced modeling, and reviewed a banking system case study.

Quiz:

1. Name three key entities in a finance data model.

2. What is the primary relationship between Customers and Accounts?

3. How is the Account-Transaction relationship structured?

4. Describe the importance of compliance in financial data modeling.

Michael E. Kirshteyn, Ph.D

With a comprehensive understanding of finance data modeling, you're prepared to design systems that support banking operations while maintaining regulatory compliance and data security.

Chapter 10: Data Modeling for the Education Industry

Overview of Education Data Needs: Student Records, Courses, and Learning Analytics

The education sector relies heavily on data to manage student records, course information, faculty details, and increasingly, learning analytics. Educational institutions, from K-12 schools to universities, need accurate and secure data models to support academic progress tracking, curriculum management, and regulatory compliance. Educational data models help institutions effectively manage student records, improve learning outcomes, and streamline administrative tasks.

In this chapter, we cover essential data modeling components for the education industry, focusing on key entities, relationships, and structures vital for managing students, courses, and educational performance analytics.

Key Entities: Students, Courses, Grades, Teachers, Enrollments

The foundation of an education data model includes several core entities that capture essential data about students, courses, and academic performance. Below are the primary entities in an education data model and their key attributes:

1. **Students**

   Represents enrolled individuals at an institution, storing personal details, enrollment information, and academic records.

   - **StudentID** (Primary Key): Unique identifier for each student.

   - **FullName**: Student's full name.

   - **DateOfBirth**: Student's date of birth.

   - **Email**: Student's email address.

   - **EnrollmentStatus**: Current enrollment status (e.g., Active, Graduated).

   - **EnrollmentDate**: Date when the student enrolled in the institution.

2. Courses

Represents courses offered by the institution, including details about course structure and schedules.

- **CourseID** (Primary Key): Unique identifier for each course.

- **CourseName**: Name of the course.

- **Credits**: Number of credits earned upon completion.

- **Department**: Department offering the course.

- **SemesterOffered**: Semester or term in which the course is available.

3. Grades

Stores the academic performance of students in specific courses.

- **GradeID** (Primary Key): Unique identifier for each grade record.

- **StudentID** (Foreign Key): Links to the student receiving the grade.

- **CourseID** (Foreign Key): Links to the course for which the grade is given.

- **Grade**: Letter or numerical grade.

- **GradeDate**: Date when the grade was assigned.

4. Teachers

Represents faculty members responsible for teaching courses.

- **TeacherID** (Primary Key): Unique identifier for each teacher.

- **FullName**: Teacher's full name.

- **Email**: Teacher's institutional email address.

- **Department**: Department to which the teacher is assigned.

- **HireDate**: Date the teacher was hired.

5. Enrollments

Manages the enrollment of students in courses each semester.

- **EnrollmentID** (Primary Key): Unique identifier for each enrollment record.

- **StudentID** (Foreign Key): Links to the enrolled student.

- **CourseID** (Foreign Key): Links to the enrolled course.

- **EnrollmentDate**: Date of enrollment in the course.

- **Status**: Enrollment status (e.g., Enrolled, Completed, Withdrawn).

Building the Education Conceptual Model

The education conceptual model establishes foundational entities and relationships necessary for student and course management. Key relationships include:

- **Student-Course Relationship**: Students enroll in multiple courses each semester, forming a many-to-many (M:N) relationship that is managed through the Enrollments entity.

- **Course-Teacher Relationship**: Each course is typically taught by one teacher, forming a one-to-many (1:M) relationship.

- **Student-Grade Relationship**: A student can have multiple grades, one for each course taken, forming a one-to-many (1:M) relationship.

This conceptual model supports student tracking, course administration, and academic performance analysis.

Subject Areas: Student Records, Course Management, Learning Analytics

1. Student Records

Manages information about students' personal details, enrollment history, and academic performance.

- **Entities**: Students, Grades, Enrollments.

- **Primary Relationships**: Student to Enrollment (1:M), Student to Grade (1:M).

- **Attributes**: Enrollment date, course grade, and enrollment status.

2. **Course Management**

Focuses on handling courses, their scheduling, and assigned teachers.

- **Entities**: Courses, Teachers, Enrollments.
- **Primary Relationships**: Course to Teacher (1:M), Course to Enrollment (M:N via Enrollments).
- **Attributes**: Course name, credits, department, semester offered.

3. **Learning Analytics**

Involves tracking and analyzing academic performance data to improve educational outcomes.

- **Entities**: Students, Grades, Courses.
- **Primary Relationships**: Student to Grade (1:M), Course to Grade (1:M).
- **Attributes**: Grade, grade date, performance metrics.

Defining Relationships and Cardinality in Education Models

Education data models often include complex relationships due to the many interactions among students, courses, grades, and teachers:

- **Student-Enrollment Relationship**: A student can enroll in multiple courses (many-to-many) through the Enrollments entity.

- **Course-Teacher Relationship**: Each course is associated with one teacher, forming a one-to-many (1:M) relationship.

- **Student-Grade Relationship**: Each student has multiple grades across different courses, creating a one-to-many (1:M) relationship.

These relationships ensure efficient tracking and management of academic and administrative data.

Logical Data Model for the Education Industry

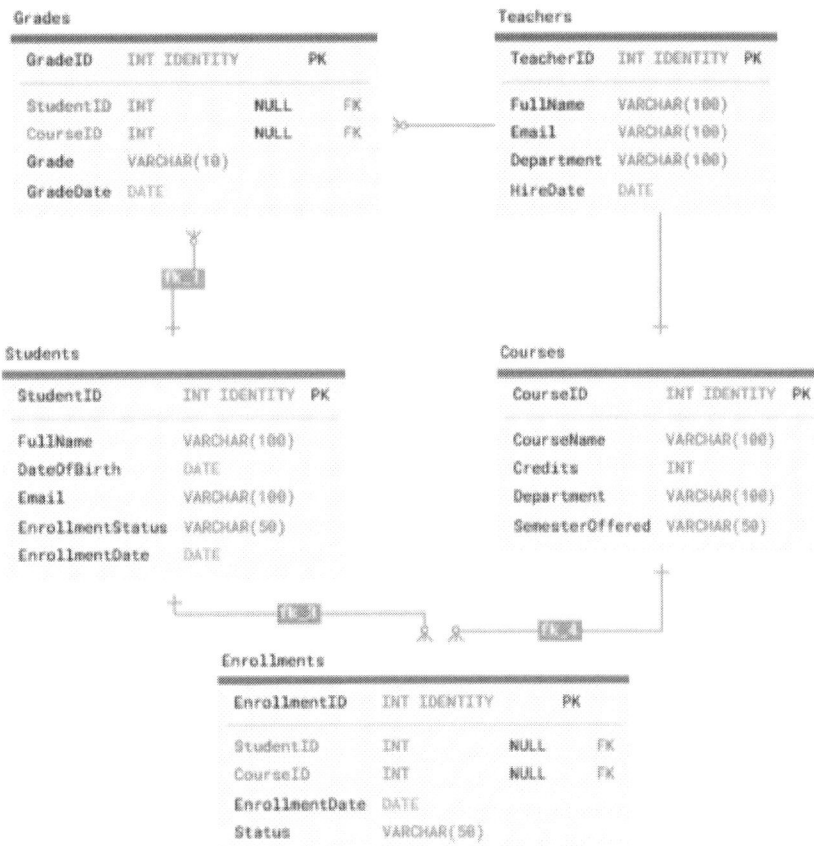

DDL for Student-Course Relationships

-- Students Table

CREATE TABLE Students (

    StudentID INT IDENTITY(1,1) PRIMARY KEY,

    FullName VARCHAR(100) NOT NULL,

    DateOfBirth DATE NOT NULL,

    Email VARCHAR(100) NOT NULL,

    EnrollmentStatus VARCHAR(50) NOT NULL,

    EnrollmentDate DATE NOT NULL

);

```
-- Courses Table
CREATE TABLE Courses (
    CourseID INT IDENTITY(1,1) PRIMARY KEY,
    CourseName VARCHAR(100) NOT NULL,
    Credits INT NOT NULL,
    [Department] VARCHAR(100) NOT NULL,
    SemesterOffered VARCHAR(50) NOT NULL
);


-- Grades Table
CREATE TABLE Grades (
    GradeID INT IDENTITY(1,1) PRIMARY KEY,
    StudentID INT FOREIGN KEY REFERENCES Students(StudentID),
    CourseID INT FOREIGN KEY REFERENCES Courses(CourseID),
    Grade VARCHAR(10) NOT NULL,
    GradeDate DATE NOT NULL
);


-- Teachers Table
CREATE TABLE Teachers (
    TeacherID INT IDENTITY(1,1) PRIMARY KEY,
    FullName VARCHAR(100) NOT NULL,
    Email VARCHAR(100) NOT NULL,
    [Department] VARCHAR(100) NOT NULL,
    HireDate DATE NOT NULL
);


-- Enrollments Table
CREATE TABLE Enrollments (
```

EnrollmentID INT IDENTITY(1,1) PRIMARY KEY,

StudentID INT FOREIGN KEY REFERENCES Students(StudentID),

CourseID INT FOREIGN KEY REFERENCES Courses(CourseID),

EnrollmentDate DATE NOT NULL,

[Status] VARCHAR(50) NOT NULL

);

Exercise: Modeling Student-Course Relationships

In this exercise, you'll create a data model representing the relationships between students, courses, and enrollments.

Steps:

1. **Define Keys and Attributes**: Identify the primary keys for each entity and define foreign keys linking them.

2. **Establish Relationships**: Map out the relationships and cardinalities between students, courses, and enrollments.

3. **Diagram Creation**: Draw a conceptual model to visualize the relationships and cardinalities.

This exercise will provide hands-on experience in defining relationships and structuring data for educational systems.

Case Study: Data Model for a University

Consider a university system that tracks student records, manages courses, and processes grades. Key model features include:

1. Student Records Management

Tracks detailed information on students, including demographics, contact information, and enrollment history. Each student record links to grades and course enrollments.

2. Course Management

Handles course details, scheduling, and teacher assignments. This allows administrators to efficiently manage course offerings each semester.

3. Academic Performance and Learning Analytics

Collects and analyzes grades to evaluate student performance, helping the institution improve academic outcomes. This data model supports grade tracking across different courses for each student.

This case study demonstrates a comprehensive educational data model designed to streamline university operations, from enrollment to academic performance analysis.

Chapter Summary and Quiz

In this chapter, we examined data modeling in the education industry, focusing on student records, course management, and learning analytics. We discussed core entities like students, courses, grades, and enrollments, as well as the complex relationships essential to managing educational data.

Quiz:

1. Name three key entities in an education data model.

2. What type of relationship exists between Students and Enrollments?

3. How is the relationship between Courses and Teachers typically structured?

4. What purpose does the Learning Analytics subject area serve?

With this foundational understanding, you're now equipped to design data models that support educational data management and improve learning outcomes.

Michael E. Kirshteyn, Ph.D

Chapter 11: Data Modeling for the Transportation and Logistics Industry

Overview of Transportation Data Needs: Fleet Management, Routing, and Supply Chain Data

The transportation and logistics industry relies on complex data structures to manage fleets, optimize routes, and track shipments across supply chains. Data models in this industry support operations like tracking vehicle maintenance, monitoring driver activity, managing shipments, and coordinating with logistics providers. A well-structured model is essential for ensuring timely deliveries, reducing operational costs, and maintaining regulatory compliance.

In this chapter, we'll cover the fundamentals of building a data model for the transportation industry, with a focus on entities that support fleet management, routing, and supply chain logistics.

Key Entities: Vehicles, Routes, Drivers, Shipments, Logistics Providers

A robust data model for transportation and logistics centers around several core entities. Below are the primary entities and their attributes:

1. **Vehicles**

Represents individual vehicles in a fleet, including operational and maintenance information.

- **VehicleID** (Primary Key): Unique identifier for each vehicle.

- **Type**: Type of vehicle (e.g., truck, van, container).

- **Capacity**: Storage or passenger capacity.

- **LicensePlate**: Vehicle's license plate number.

- **Status**: Current status (e.g., Active, In Maintenance).

- **LastMaintenanceDate**: Date of the last maintenance check.

2. Routes

Defines the paths vehicles travel, including start and end locations, distances, and estimated times.

- **RouteID** (Primary Key): Unique identifier for each route.

- **StartLocation**: Starting point of the route.

- **EndLocation**: Endpoint of the route.

- **Distance**: Distance of the route in miles or kilometers.

- **EstimatedTime**: Estimated time to complete the route.

3. Drivers

Represents the drivers responsible for transporting shipments.

- **DriverID** (Primary Key): Unique identifier for each driver.

- **FullName**: Driver's full name.

- **LicenseNumber**: Driver's license number.

- **LicenseType**: Type of license (e.g., commercial, heavy vehicle).

- **HireDate**: Date the driver was hired.

- **Status**: Driver's current status (e.g., Active, In Training).

4. Shipments

Manages details about individual shipments, including origin, destination, and shipment status.

- **ShipmentID** (Primary Key): Unique identifier for each shipment.

- **Origin**: Starting point of the shipment.

- **Destination**: Endpoint of the shipment.

- **Weight**: Total weight of the shipment.

- **Status**: Shipment status (e.g., In Transit, Delivered, Pending).

- **PickupDate**: Date the shipment was picked up.

- **DeliveryDate**: Expected or actual delivery date.

5. Logistics Providers

Represents external logistics partners or third-party service providers.

- **ProviderID** (Primary Key): Unique identifier for each provider.

- **ProviderName**: Name of the logistics provider.

- **ContactInfo**: Contact details of the provider.

- **ServiceArea**: Geographic area covered by the provider.

- **ServiceType**: Type of logistics service (e.g., warehousing, transportation).

Constructing the Transportation and Logistics Conceptual Model

In the transportation and logistics data model, essential relationships capture the interactions between vehicles, drivers, shipments, and routes. Key relationships include:

- **Vehicle-Driver Relationship**: Each vehicle is assigned to one driver per trip, forming a one-to-one (1:1) relationship.

- **Driver-Shipment Relationship**: Drivers may transport multiple shipments, resulting in a one-to-many (1:M) relationship.

- **Shipment-Route Relationship**: Shipments are transported over specific routes, establishing a many-to-one (M:1) relationship.

This conceptual model serves as a foundation for fleet management, route planning, and shipment tracking, supporting the efficient movement of goods through the supply chain.

Subject Areas: Fleet Management, Route Optimization, Shipment Tracking

1. Fleet Management

Covers the vehicles and drivers required to transport goods, including maintenance and assignment data.

Michael E. Kirshteyn, Ph.D

111

- **Entities**: Vehicles, Drivers.

- **Primary Relationships**: Vehicle to Driver (1:1).

- **Attributes**: Vehicle status, driver details, maintenance records.

2. Route Optimization

Manages route planning, distance tracking, and estimated travel times to optimize delivery efficiency.

- **Entities**: Routes, Vehicles.

- **Primary Relationships**: Vehicle to Route (1:M).

- **Attributes**: Route distance, start and end locations, estimated time.

3. Shipment Tracking

Tracks shipments throughout their journey, from origin to destination, and monitors delivery status.

- **Entities**: Shipments, Routes, Logistics Providers.

- **Primary Relationships**: Shipment to Route (M:1), Shipment to Provider (M:1).

- **Attributes**: Shipment origin and destination, status, weight, and provider details.

Relationship Derivation and Cardinality in Transportation Models

Transportation data models include complex relationships due to the dynamic nature of fleet operations and logistics:

- **Vehicle to Driver**: One driver is assigned per vehicle per trip, creating a one-to-one (1:1) relationship.

- **Driver to Shipment**: A driver can manage multiple shipments within one route, forming a one-to-many (1:M) relationship.

- **Shipment to Route**: Multiple shipments can travel along the same route, establishing a many-to-one (M:1) relationship.

Understanding these relationships helps ensure accurate tracking of resources, shipments, and personnel within the transportation model.

Logical Model for the Transportation and Logistics Industry

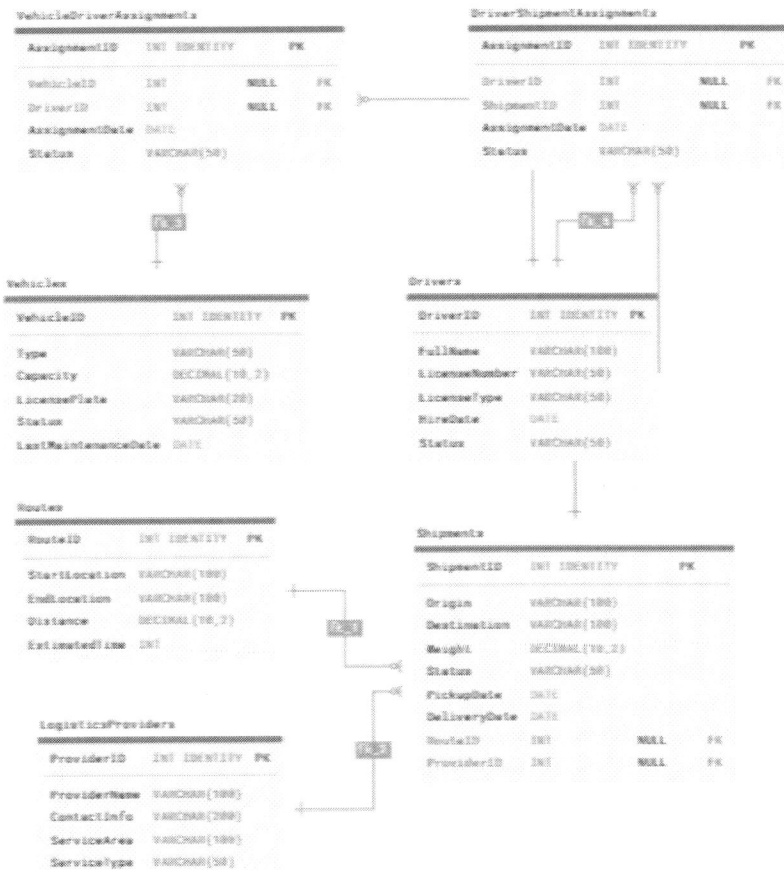

DDL for Transportation and Logistics Industry

-- Vehicles Table

CREATE TABLE Vehicles (

    VehicleID INT IDENTITY(1,1) PRIMARY KEY,

    [Type] VARCHAR(50) NOT NULL,

```sql
    Capacity DECIMAL(10,2) NOT NULL,

    LicensePlate VARCHAR(20) NOT NULL,

    [Status] VARCHAR(50) NOT NULL,

    LastMaintenanceDate DATE NOT NULL
);


-- Routes Table
CREATE TABLE Routes (

    RouteID INT IDENTITY(1,1) PRIMARY KEY,

    StartLocation VARCHAR(100) NOT NULL,

    EndLocation VARCHAR(100) NOT NULL,

    Distance DECIMAL(10,2) NOT NULL,

    EstimatedTime INT NOT NULL  -- In minutes
);


-- Drivers Table
CREATE TABLE Drivers (

    DriverID INT IDENTITY(1,1) PRIMARY KEY,

    FullName VARCHAR(100) NOT NULL,

    LicenseNumber VARCHAR(50) NOT NULL,

    LicenseType VARCHAR(50) NOT NULL,

    HireDate DATE NOT NULL,

    [Status] VARCHAR(50) NOT NULL
);


-- Logistics Providers Table
CREATE TABLE LogisticsProviders (

    ProviderID INT IDENTITY(1,1) PRIMARY KEY,

    ProviderName VARCHAR(100) NOT NULL,

    ContactInfo VARCHAR(200) NOT NULL,
```

```
ServiceArea VARCHAR(100) NOT NULL,

ServiceType VARCHAR(50) NOT NULL

);


-- Shipments Table

CREATE TABLE Shipments (

    ShipmentID INT IDENTITY(1,1) PRIMARY KEY,

    Origin VARCHAR(100) NOT NULL,

    Destination VARCHAR(100) NOT NULL,

    Weight DECIMAL(10,2) NOT NULL,

    [Status] VARCHAR(50) NOT NULL,

    PickupDate DATE NOT NULL,

    DeliveryDate DATE NOT NULL,

    RouteID INT FOREIGN KEY REFERENCES Routes(RouteID),

    ProviderID INT FOREIGN KEY REFERENCES LogisticsProviders(ProviderID)

);


-- Vehicle-Driver Assignment Bridge Table (for 1:1 relationship per trip)

CREATE TABLE VehicleDriverAssignments (

    AssignmentID INT IDENTITY(1,1) PRIMARY KEY,

    VehicleID INT FOREIGN KEY REFERENCES Vehicles(VehicleID),

    DriverID INT FOREIGN KEY REFERENCES Drivers(DriverID),

    AssignmentDate DATE NOT NULL,

    [Status] VARCHAR(50) NOT NULL,

    CONSTRAINT UQ_ActiveAssignment UNIQUE (VehicleID, DriverID, AssignmentDate)

);


-- Driver-Shipment Assignment Bridge Table (for 1:M relationship)

CREATE TABLE DriverShipmentAssignments (

    AssignmentID INT IDENTITY(1,1) PRIMARY KEY,
```

DriverID INT FOREIGN KEY REFERENCES Drivers(DriverID),

ShipmentID INT FOREIGN KEY REFERENCES Shipments(ShipmentID),

AssignmentDate DATE NOT NULL,

[Status] VARCHAR(50) NOT NULL

);

Exercise: Modeling Vehicle and Shipment Relationships

In this exercise, you'll design a model for tracking vehicles and shipments along their routes.

Steps:

1. **Define Entities**: Outline the primary entities—vehicles, drivers, routes, and shipments.

2. **Establish Keys and Attributes**: Identify primary and foreign keys and assign attributes to each entity.

3. **Derive Relationships**: Create relationships between entities, including cardinalities for Vehicle-Driver, Driver-Shipment, and Shipment-Route.

This exercise will enhance your ability to model relationships essential for managing transportation resources and shipments.

Case Study: Data Model for a Logistics Provider

Consider a logistics company that transports goods across multiple regions. Key model features include:

1. Fleet and Driver Management

Tracks details on all vehicles, including maintenance history and driver assignments. Each vehicle is assigned a driver, ensuring accountability and efficiency.

2. Route Planning and Optimization

Maintains a record of standard routes, distances, and estimated travel times to help optimize deliveries and reduce fuel costs. Each route has an assigned start and end location to streamline navigation.

3. Shipment and Status Tracking

Manages details on shipments, including origin, destination, weight, and delivery status. Shipments are tracked through each route leg and linked to specific logistics providers for end-to-end visibility.

This case study highlights a comprehensive model for managing logistics operations, tracking shipments, and optimizing fleet utilization.

Chapter Summary and Quiz

In this chapter, we explored data modeling in the transportation and logistics industry, covering fleet management, route optimization, and shipment tracking. Key entities like vehicles, drivers, shipments, and routes play a central role in transportation models, facilitating efficient logistics operations and supply chain management.

Quiz:

1. Name three key entities in a transportation data model.

2. What type of relationship exists between Drivers and Shipments?

3. Which entity is typically used to manage multiple routes?

4. How does route optimization support logistics operations?

With this knowledge, you're now prepared to design data models that support efficient transportation and logistics operations in a range of business contexts.

Chapter 12: Data Modeling for the Energy and Utilities Industry

Industry Overview: Asset Management, Consumption Data, and Compliance

In the energy and utilities industry, data models are essential for managing infrastructure, tracking energy consumption, ensuring accurate billing, and maintaining compliance with regulatory requirements. Models must support diverse operations, such as monitoring assets, managing grid operations, and handling customer billing. Energy providers rely on these models to ensure efficient resource distribution, effective infrastructure management, and timely invoicing.

This chapter will guide you through developing a data model for the energy and utilities sector, focusing on key entities and the relationships that support operations in asset management, consumption tracking, and billing.

Key Entities: Energy Assets, Consumers, Consumption, Billing, Grid Management

A comprehensive data model for energy and utilities includes several core entities. Here are the primary entities and their associated attributes:

1. **Energy Assets**

   Represents the infrastructure required for generating, storing, and distributing energy (e.g., power plants, transformers).

   - **AssetID** (Primary Key): Unique identifier for each energy asset.

   - **Type**: Type of asset (e.g., generator, substation, transformer).

   - **Location**: Physical location of the asset.

   - **Status**: Current operational status (e.g., Active, Maintenance).

   - **Capacity**: Capacity or output level of the asset.

   - **InstallationDate**: Date the asset was installed.

2. **Consumers**

Represents the customers or entities that consume energy.

- **ConsumerID** (Primary Key): Unique identifier for each consumer.

- **ConsumerType**: Type of consumer (e.g., residential, commercial, industrial).

- **Location**: Address or service location of the consumer.

- **Status**: Customer status (e.g., Active, Inactive).

- **ContactInfo**: Contact details of the consumer.

3. **Consumption**

Tracks energy usage for each consumer, typically measured through a metering device.

- **ConsumptionID** (Primary Key): Unique identifier for each consumption record.

- **ConsumerID** (Foreign Key): Identifier for the related consumer.

- **MeterID**: Identifier for the meter device used for measurement.

- **Date**: Date of consumption measurement.

- **UsageAmount**: Amount of energy consumed.

- **Unit**: Unit of measurement (e.g., kWh, therms).

4. **Billing**

Handles billing information related to energy consumption, including charges and due dates.

- **BillID** (Primary Key): Unique identifier for each bill.

- **ConsumerID** (Foreign Key): Identifier for the related consumer.

- **BillingPeriod**: Period for which the bill applies.

- **AmountDue**: Total amount due.

- **DueDate**: Due date for the bill.

- **Status**: Bill status (e.g., Paid, Unpaid, Overdue).

5. **Grid Management**

Manages data related to grid infrastructure, including grid segments and power flow details.

- **GridSegmentID** (Primary Key): Unique identifier for each grid segment.

- **StartPoint**: Starting point of the grid segment.

- **EndPoint**: Endpoint of the grid segment.

- **Capacity**: Capacity of the segment.

- **CurrentLoad**: Current load on the segment.

- **Status**: Operational status of the segment.

Constructing the Conceptual Model for Energy and Utilities

In the energy and utilities data model, relationships among these entities enable critical functions such as consumption tracking, billing, and grid management. Key relationships include:

- **Consumer-Consumption Relationship**: Each consumer has multiple consumption records, forming a one-to-many (1:M) relationship.

- **Consumer-Billing Relationship**: Each consumer has multiple billing records, also creating a one-to-many (1:M) relationship.

- **Consumption-Grid Segment Relationship**: Consumption data is linked to specific grid segments to monitor load and usage patterns.

This conceptual model supports energy providers in monitoring infrastructure usage, billing customers accurately, and managing grid reliability.

Subject Areas: Consumption Management, Billing, Grid Operations

1. **Consumption Management**

Focuses on tracking energy usage by consumers and monitoring the load on grid assets.

- **Entities**: Consumers, Consumption, Grid Management.

- **Primary Relationships**: Consumer to Consumption (1:M).

- **Attributes**: Usage amount, measurement date, consumer location.

2. Billing

Manages customer invoicing based on consumption data and ensures timely payment tracking.

- **Entities**: Consumers, Billing, Consumption.

- **Primary Relationships**: Consumer to Billing (1:M), Consumption to Billing (M:1).

- **Attributes**: Billing period, amount due, due date, billing status.

3. Grid Operations

Monitors the energy grid infrastructure, including segments, load, and distribution, to ensure reliable energy delivery.

- **Entities**: Grid Management, Energy Assets.

- **Primary Relationships**: Asset to Grid Segment (1:M).

- **Attributes**: Grid segment capacity, current load, asset location.

Cardinality and Relationships in Energy Models

The data model for energy and utilities includes complex relationships due to the industry's reliance on infrastructure and consumption tracking:

- **Consumer to Consumption**: Each consumer can have multiple consumption records, resulting in a one-to-many (1:M) relationship.

- **Consumer to Billing**: Consumers may receive multiple bills over time, forming a one-to-many (1:M) relationship.

- **Consumption to Grid Segment**: Consumption may be associated with specific grid segments, creating a many-to-one (M:1) relationship.

These relationships enable tracking of energy usage, billing, and infrastructure load distribution effectively within the energy and utilities model.

Logical Data Model for the Energy and Utilities Industry

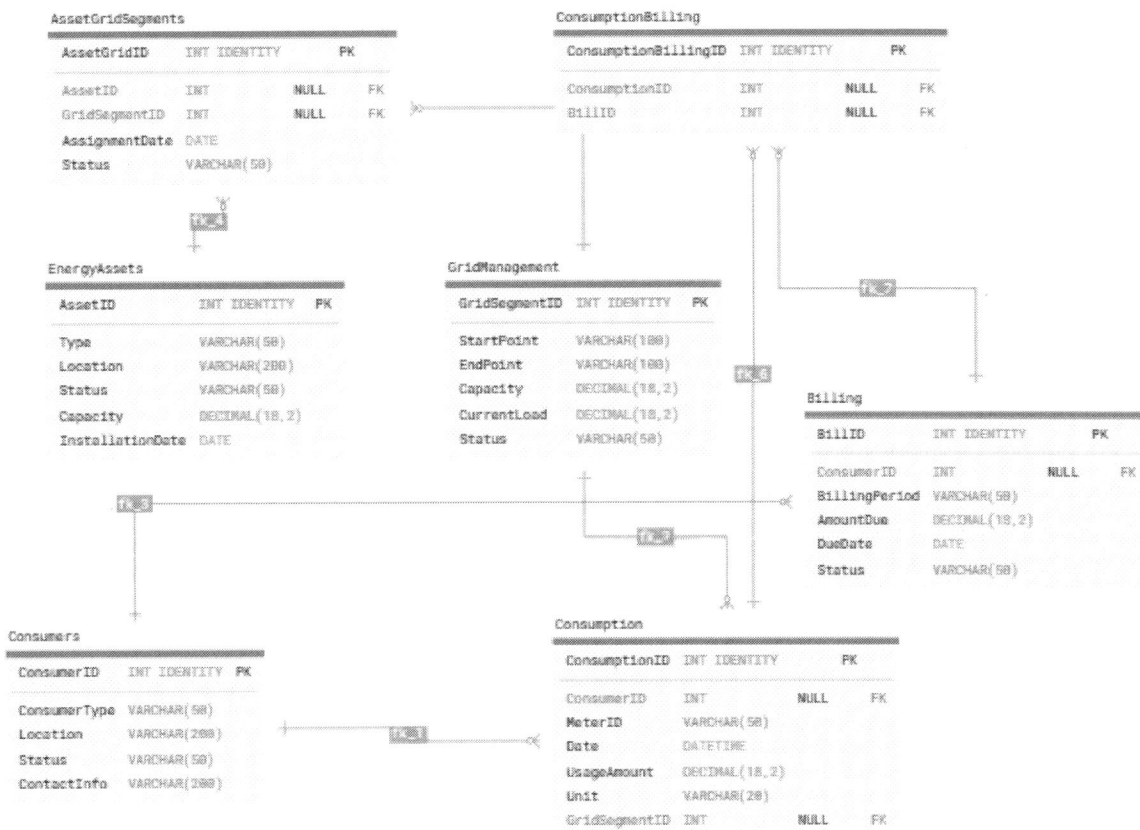

DDL for Energy and Utilities Industry

-- Energy Assets Table

CREATE TABLE EnergyAssets (

```
    AssetID INT IDENTITY(1,1) PRIMARY KEY,

    [Type] VARCHAR(50) NOT NULL,

    Location VARCHAR(200) NOT NULL,

    [Status] VARCHAR(50) NOT NULL,

    Capacity DECIMAL(18,2) NOT NULL,

    InstallationDate DATE NOT NULL
);


-- Consumers Table
CREATE TABLE Consumers (

    ConsumerID INT IDENTITY(1,1) PRIMARY KEY,

    ConsumerType VARCHAR(50) NOT NULL,

    Location VARCHAR(200) NOT NULL,

    [Status] VARCHAR(50) NOT NULL,

    ContactInfo VARCHAR(200) NOT NULL
);


-- Grid Management Table
CREATE TABLE GridManagement (

    GridSegmentID INT IDENTITY(1,1) PRIMARY KEY,

    StartPoint VARCHAR(100) NOT NULL,

    EndPoint VARCHAR(100) NOT NULL,

    Capacity DECIMAL(18,2) NOT NULL,

    CurrentLoad DECIMAL(18,2) NOT NULL,

    [Status] VARCHAR(50) NOT NULL
);


-- Consumption Table
CREATE TABLE Consumption (

    ConsumptionID INT IDENTITY(1,1) PRIMARY KEY,
```

```
    ConsumerID INT FOREIGN KEY REFERENCES Consumers(ConsumerID),

    MeterID VARCHAR(50) NOT NULL,

    [Date] DATETIME NOT NULL,

    UsageAmount DECIMAL(18,2) NOT NULL,

    Unit VARCHAR(20) NOT NULL,

    GridSegmentID INT FOREIGN KEY REFERENCES GridManagement(GridSegmentID)
);


-- Billing Table
CREATE TABLE Billing (

    BillID INT IDENTITY(1,1) PRIMARY KEY,

    ConsumerID INT FOREIGN KEY REFERENCES Consumers(ConsumerID),

    BillingPeriod VARCHAR(50) NOT NULL,

    AmountDue DECIMAL(18,2) NOT NULL,

    DueDate DATE NOT NULL,

    [Status] VARCHAR(50) NOT NULL
);


-- Asset-Grid Segment Bridge Table (for 1:M relationship)
CREATE TABLE AssetGridSegments (

    AssetGridID INT IDENTITY(1,1) PRIMARY KEY,

    AssetID INT FOREIGN KEY REFERENCES EnergyAssets(AssetID),

    GridSegmentID INT FOREIGN KEY REFERENCES GridManagement(GridSegmentID),

    AssignmentDate DATE NOT NULL,

    [Status] VARCHAR(50) NOT NULL
);


-- Consumption-Billing Bridge Table (for M:1 relationship)
CREATE TABLE ConsumptionBilling (

    ConsumptionBillingID INT IDENTITY(1,1) PRIMARY KEY,
```

```
ConsumptionID INT FOREIGN KEY REFERENCES Consumption(ConsumptionID),

BillID INT FOREIGN KEY REFERENCES Billing(BillID),

CONSTRAINT UQ_ConsumptionBill UNIQUE (ConsumptionID, BillID)
);
```

```
-- Create indexes for frequently accessed columns
CREATE INDEX IX_Consumption_ConsumerID ON Consumption(ConsumerID);

CREATE INDEX IX_Consumption_Date ON Consumption([Date]);

CREATE INDEX IX_Billing_ConsumerID ON Billing(ConsumerID);

CREATE INDEX IX_Billing_Status ON Billing([Status]);

CREATE INDEX IX_GridManagement_Status ON GridManagement([Status]);
```

Exercise: Modeling Metering and Billing Relationships

In this exercise, you'll develop a data model for tracking metering and billing details for energy consumers.

Steps:

1. **Define Entities**: Identify the primary entities—Consumers, Consumption, Billing, and Meters.

2. **Establish Keys and Attributes**: Specify primary and foreign keys for each entity and define attributes.

3. **Derive Relationships**: Create relationships between entities, focusing on cardinalities for Consumer-Consumption, Consumer-Billing, and Consumption-Grid Segment.

This exercise will enhance your skills in modeling relationships that support accurate consumption tracking and billing processes.

Case Study: Data Model for an Energy Provider

Consider an energy provider responsible for delivering electricity to residential and commercial customers. Key features of the model include:

1. **Asset and Grid Management**

Tracks information on energy assets, such as substations and transformers, and monitors grid load and capacity for optimal performance.

2. **Consumption Monitoring**

Records energy usage for each customer, with data collected from meters and associated with specific grid segments.

3. **Billing Management**

Generates bills based on usage data and manages payment status, billing cycles, and overdue payments for each consumer.

This case study highlights a comprehensive approach to managing energy data, from infrastructure tracking to customer billing.

Chapter Summary and Quiz

In this chapter, we examined data modeling for the energy and utilities industry, with a focus on entities like energy assets, consumers, consumption records, billing, and grid management. Data models in this sector support crucial functions like asset monitoring, energy consumption tracking, and billing processes.

Quiz:

1. List three key entities in a data model for the energy and utilities industry.

2. What type of relationship exists between Consumers and Consumption?

3. How is consumption data linked to grid segments in a data model?

4. What is a primary purpose of the Billing entity in an energy model?

With these fundamentals, you're now prepared to design models that support critical operations in the energy and utilities industry, enabling efficient resource management and reliable service delivery.

Chapter 13: Data Modeling for the Public Sector and Government

Overview of Public Sector Data Needs: Citizen Data, Public Services, and Administration

Data modeling in the public sector supports diverse services provided by government agencies, including citizen data management, public services administration, and benefits distribution. Due to the sensitive nature of government data, public sector data models must account for privacy regulations and access controls. These models often integrate various data sources and track a wide range of interactions, such as citizen services, policy management, and public benefits.

This chapter will explore the essential components of a data model tailored for the public sector, focusing on the entities and relationships that support efficient government service delivery.

Key Entities: Citizens, Public Services, Benefits, Employees, Government Policies

In public sector data modeling, key entities capture information about citizens, the services they access, and government resources. Here's a look at the primary entities and their attributes:

1. **Citizens**

   Represents individuals who are recipients of government services.

   - **CitizenID** (Primary Key): Unique identifier for each citizen.

   - **FullName**: Full name of the citizen.

   - **DateOfBirth**: Date of birth.

   - **Address**: Residential address.

   - **ContactInfo**: Contact details, including phone and email.

   - **Status**: Active or inactive status regarding public services.

2. **Public Services**

Catalogs services offered by government agencies, such as healthcare, education, and transportation.

- **ServiceID** (Primary Key): Unique identifier for each public service.

- **ServiceName**: Name of the service.

- **Department**: Department responsible for providing the service.

- **EligibilityCriteria**: Requirements for citizens to qualify.

- **ServiceCost**: Cost, if any, associated with the service.

3. **Benefits**

Details benefits provided to eligible citizens, such as financial assistance, healthcare benefits, or educational grants.

- **BenefitID** (Primary Key): Unique identifier for each benefit.

- **BenefitType**: Type of benefit (e.g., housing, healthcare, education).

- **EligibilityRequirements**: Requirements for receiving the benefit.

- **Amount**: Financial amount associated with the benefit, if applicable.

- **BenefitStatus**: Status (e.g., Approved, Pending, Denied).

4. **Employees**

Tracks government employees who administer services and manage citizen interactions.

- **EmployeeID** (Primary Key): Unique identifier for each employee.

- **Name**: Name of the employee.

- **Position**: Job title.

- **Department**: Department to which the employee is assigned.

- **ContactInfo**: Contact details for communication.

5. **Government Policies**

Contains information on policies that influence public services and citizen benefits.

- **PolicyID** (Primary Key): Unique identifier for each policy.

- **PolicyName**: Name of the policy.

- **Description**: Description and purpose of the policy.

- **EffectiveDate**: Date the policy goes into effect.

- **Department**: Department responsible for enforcing the policy.

Building the Public Sector Conceptual Model

The conceptual model for the public sector includes relationships among citizens, the services they use, the benefits they receive, and the employees who administer these services. Core relationships include:

- **Citizen-Benefits Relationship**: Citizens may receive multiple benefits, forming a one-to-many (1:M) relationship.

- **Citizen-Public Services Relationship**: Citizens may access various public services, resulting in a many-to-many (M:N) relationship, where a citizen can access multiple services and each service may be used by multiple citizens.

- **Employees-Services Relationship**: Each service may involve multiple employees who help administer it, creating a many-to-many (M:N) relationship.

This model supports government operations by facilitating efficient citizen service management, benefit distribution, and policy enforcement.

Subject Areas: Citizen Management, Benefits Administration, Government Services

1. Citizen Management

Focuses on tracking information related to citizens, including their status and interactions with government services.

- **Entities**: Citizens, Public Services, Benefits.

- **Primary Relationships**: Citizen to Benefits (1:M), Citizen to Services (M:N).

- **Attributes**: Citizen status, eligibility, contact information.

2. Benefits Administration

Manages benefit allocation and eligibility requirements for citizens.

- **Entities**: Citizens, Benefits, Policies.

- **Primary Relationships**: Citizen to Benefits (1:M), Policies to Benefits (1:M).

- **Attributes**: Benefit eligibility, benefit type, amount, policy influence.

3. Government Services

Supports administration and monitoring of public services, including employee involvement and policy impact.

- **Entities**: Public Services, Employees, Policies.

- **Primary Relationships**: Service to Employee (M:N), Service to Policy (M:N).

- **Attributes**: Service eligibility, department, employee roles.

Relationship Derivation and Cardinality in Public Sector Models

Key relationships in the public sector data model help connect citizens with the services and benefits they are eligible for and track interactions among employees and services:

- **Citizen to Benefits**: Citizens can receive multiple benefits, resulting in a one-to-many (1:M) relationship.

- **Citizen to Public Services**: Citizens access various public services, leading to a many-to-many (M:N) relationship through a junction entity, such as ServiceEnrolment.

- **Service to Employee**: Each public service may have multiple employees administering it, forming a many-to-many (M:M) relationship.

These relationships support the complex administrative needs of public sector organizations.

Logical Data Model for the Public Sector and Government

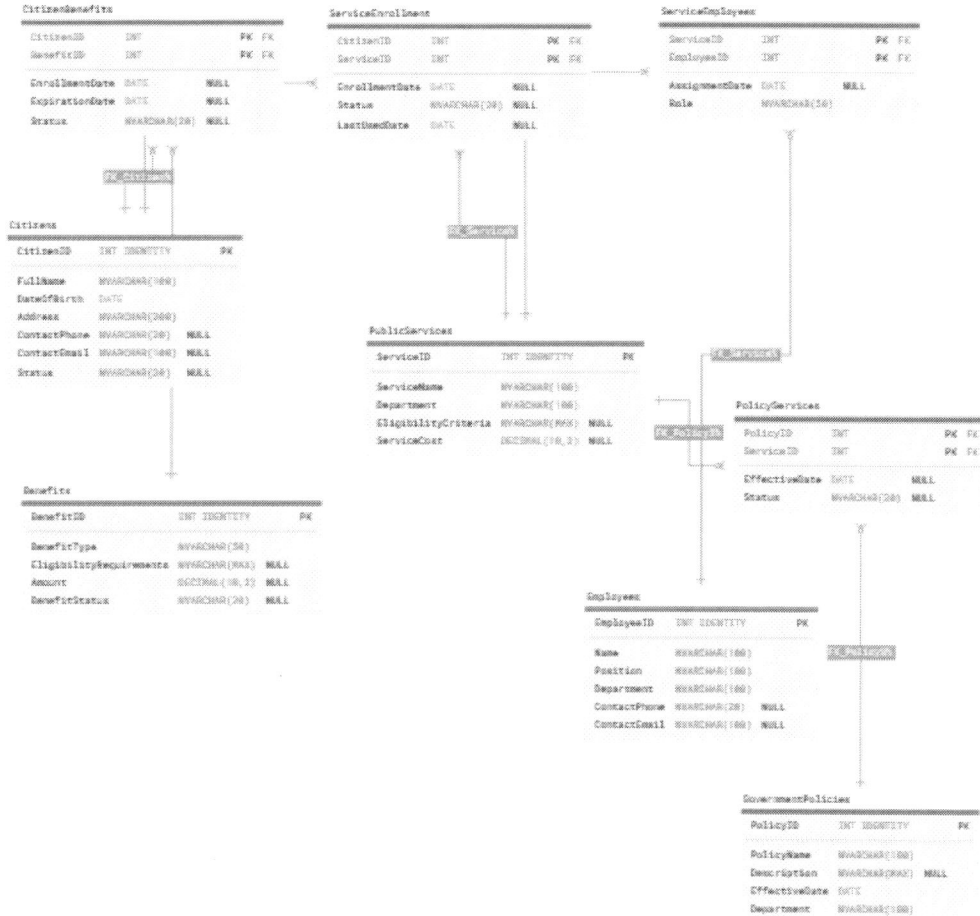

DDL for Public Sector and Government

-- Create Citizens table

CREATE TABLE Citizens (

```
    CitizenID INT PRIMARY KEY IDENTITY(1,1),

    FullName NVARCHAR(100) NOT NULL,

    DateOfBirth DATE NOT NULL,

    Address NVARCHAR(200) NOT NULL,

    ContactPhone NVARCHAR(20),

    ContactEmail NVARCHAR(100),

    Status NVARCHAR(20) DEFAULT 'Active' CHECK (Status IN ('Active', 'Inactive'))
);


-- Create Public Services table
CREATE TABLE PublicServices (

    ServiceID INT PRIMARY KEY IDENTITY(1,1),

    ServiceName NVARCHAR(100) NOT NULL,

    Department NVARCHAR(100) NOT NULL,

    EligibilityCriteria NVARCHAR(MAX),

    ServiceCost DECIMAL(10,2),

    CONSTRAINT UC_ServiceName UNIQUE (ServiceName)
);


-- Create Benefits table
CREATE TABLE Benefits (

    BenefitID INT PRIMARY KEY IDENTITY(1,1),

    BenefitType NVARCHAR(50) NOT NULL,

    EligibilityRequirements NVARCHAR(MAX),

    Amount DECIMAL(10,2),

    BenefitStatus NVARCHAR(20) CHECK (BenefitStatus IN ('Approved', 'Pending', 'Denied')),

    CONSTRAINT UC_BenefitType UNIQUE (BenefitType)
);


-- Create Employees table
```

```sql
CREATE TABLE Employees (

    EmployeeID INT PRIMARY KEY IDENTITY(1,1),

    Name NVARCHAR(100) NOT NULL,

    Position NVARCHAR(100) NOT NULL,

    Department NVARCHAR(100) NOT NULL,

    ContactPhone NVARCHAR(20),

    ContactEmail NVARCHAR(100)

);


-- Create Government Policies table
CREATE TABLE GovernmentPolicies (

    PolicyID INT PRIMARY KEY IDENTITY(1,1),

    PolicyName NVARCHAR(100) NOT NULL,

    Description NVARCHAR(MAX),

    EffectiveDate DATE NOT NULL,

    Department NVARCHAR(100) NOT NULL,

    CONSTRAINT UC_PolicyName UNIQUE (PolicyName)

);


-- Create CitizenBenefits bridge table (Citizen to Benefits: 1:M)
CREATE TABLE CitizenBenefits (

    CitizenID INT,

    BenefitID INT,

    EnrollmentDate DATE DEFAULT GETDATE(),

    ExpirationDate DATE,

    Status NVARCHAR(20) DEFAULT 'Active',

    CONSTRAINT PK_CitizenBenefits PRIMARY KEY (CitizenID, BenefitID),

    CONSTRAINT FK_CitizenBenefits_Citizen FOREIGN KEY (CitizenID)

        REFERENCES Citizens(CitizenID),

    CONSTRAINT FK_CitizenBenefits_Benefit FOREIGN KEY (BenefitID)
```

```
      REFERENCES Benefits(BenefitID)
);


-- Create ServiceEnrollment bridge table (Citizen to Services: M:N)
CREATE TABLE ServiceEnrollment (
   CitizenID INT,
   ServiceID INT,
   EnrollmentDate DATE DEFAULT GETDATE(),
   Status NVARCHAR(20) DEFAULT 'Active',
   LastUsedDate DATE,
   CONSTRAINT PK_ServiceEnrollment PRIMARY KEY (CitizenID, ServiceID),
   CONSTRAINT FK_ServiceEnrollment_Citizen FOREIGN KEY (CitizenID)
      REFERENCES Citizens(CitizenID),
   CONSTRAINT FK_ServiceEnrollment_Service FOREIGN KEY (ServiceID)
      REFERENCES PublicServices(ServiceID)
);


-- Create ServiceEmployees bridge table (Service to Employees: M:N)
CREATE TABLE ServiceEmployees (
   ServiceID INT,
   EmployeeID INT,
   AssignmentDate DATE DEFAULT GETDATE(),
   Role NVARCHAR(50) NOT NULL,
   CONSTRAINT PK_ServiceEmployees PRIMARY KEY (ServiceID, EmployeeID),
   CONSTRAINT FK_ServiceEmployees_Service FOREIGN KEY (ServiceID)
      REFERENCES PublicServices(ServiceID),
   CONSTRAINT FK_ServiceEmployees_Employee FOREIGN KEY (EmployeeID)
      REFERENCES Employees(EmployeeID)
);
```

-- Create PolicyServices bridge table (Policy to Services: M:N)

```
CREATE TABLE PolicyServices (

    PolicyID INT,

    ServiceID INT,

    EffectiveDate DATE DEFAULT GETDATE(),

    Status NVARCHAR(20) DEFAULT 'Active',

    CONSTRAINT PK_PolicyServices PRIMARY KEY (PolicyID, ServiceID),

    CONSTRAINT FK_PolicyServices_Policy FOREIGN KEY (PolicyID)

        REFERENCES GovernmentPolicies(PolicyID),

    CONSTRAINT FK_PolicyServices_Service FOREIGN KEY (ServiceID)

        REFERENCES PublicServices(ServiceID)

);
```

-- Create indexes for better query performance

```
CREATE INDEX IX_Citizens_Status ON Citizens(Status);

CREATE INDEX IX_Benefits_BenefitStatus ON Benefits(BenefitStatus);

CREATE INDEX IX_ServiceEnrollment_Status ON ServiceEnrollment(Status);

CREATE INDEX IX_CitizenBenefits_Status ON CitizenBenefits(Status);

CREATE INDEX IX_PolicyServices_Status ON PolicyServices(Status);
```

Exercise: Modeling Citizen-Benefit and Government Relationships

In this exercise, you'll create a model that includes citizens, benefits, and services. Follow these steps:

1. **Define Entities**: Identify primary entities—Citizens, Benefits, Public Services.

2. **Establish Keys and Attributes**: Define primary keys, foreign keys, and additional attributes.

3. **Create Relationships**: Model relationships between entities, focusing on cardinality for Citizen-Benefit and Citizen-Service.

Case Study: Data Model for a Municipal Government

In this case study, we look at the data model for a municipal government that provides essential services to residents, such as waste management, public transportation, and housing assistance.

1. **Citizen Information**: Maintains up-to-date data on citizens, including personal details, service history, and benefit eligibility.

2. **Public Services Administration**: Manages available services and keeps track of citizen enrolment.

3. **Benefits Management**: Distributes benefits such as subsidies and grants, with eligibility determined by government policies.

The data model enables efficient management of citizen services, streamlines benefit distribution, and provides a structure for tracking service usage and compliance.

Chapter Summary and Quiz

In this chapter, we covered data modeling for the public sector, focusing on entities like citizens, public services, benefits, employees, and policies. A well-designed data model in this field supports government operations in areas such as citizen services, benefits administration, and policy compliance.

Quiz:

1. Name three key entities in a public sector data model.

2. What type of relationship exists between Citizens and Benefits?

3. How would you model the relationship between Public Services and Employees?

4. Why is it essential to track relationships between citizens and public services in the public sector?

This chapter provides a foundation for designing models that meet the needs of public sector organizations, ensuring efficient service delivery, benefits administration, and compliance with regulatory standards.

Chapter 14: Data Modeling for Hospitality and Travel

Industry Overview: Data Needs for Bookings, Reservations, and Customer Experiences

The hospitality and travel industry relies on efficient data models to manage bookings, reservations, customer data, and payments. Key data requirements include handling complex reservation systems, tracking customer preferences, and providing seamless, personalized experiences across hotels, flights, and other travel services. Data security and compliance are also critical, as sensitive information like payment details and personal data must be safeguarded.

In this chapter, we explore the essential components of a data model for hospitality and travel, focusing on the entities and relationships that enable streamlined booking, customer management, and transaction processing.

Key Entities: Customers, Reservations, Hotels, Flights, Payments

To manage customer interactions and reservations effectively, the following key entities and attributes are central to the hospitality and travel data model:

1. **Customers**

Represents individuals using hospitality or travel services.

- **CustomerID** (Primary Key): Unique identifier for each customer.

- **FullName**: Customer's full name.

- **ContactInfo**: Contact details, including email and phone number.

- **Address**: Residential address.

- **Preferences**: Customer preferences for accommodations, seating, etc.

- **LoyaltyPoints**: Points accumulated through loyalty programs.

2. Reservations

Tracks bookings for hotels, flights, or other services.

- **ReservationID** (Primary Key): Unique identifier for each reservation.

- **CustomerID** (Foreign Key): Links to the customer who made the reservation.

- **ReservationDate**: Date when the reservation was made.

- **ServiceType**: Type of reservation (e.g., hotel, flight, car rental).

- **StartDate**: Start date of the reservation.

- **EndDate**: End date of the reservation.

- **Status**: Status of the reservation (e.g., Confirmed, Pending, Cancelled).

3. Hotels

Stores information about hotels where customers make reservations.

- **HotelID** (Primary Key): Unique identifier for each hotel.

- **HotelName**: Name of the hotel.

- **Location**: Location details, including city and address.

- **Amenities**: Available amenities (e.g., pool, Wi-Fi, breakfast).

- **RoomTypes**: Types of rooms available (e.g., single, suite).

- **Capacity**: Maximum occupancy of the hotel.

4. Flights

Contains details for flights in which customers book reservations.

- **FlightID** (Primary Key): Unique identifier for each flight.

- **Airline**: Name of the airline operating the flight.

- **FlightNumber**: Designated number for the flight.

- **Departure**: Departure city and airport.

- **Destination**: Destination city and airport.

- **DepartureDateTime**: Scheduled departure date and time.

- **ArrivalDateTime**: Scheduled arrival date and time.

5. **Payments**

Manages payments associated with reservations.

- **PaymentID** (Primary Key): Unique identifier for each payment.

- **ReservationID** (Foreign Key): Links to the associated reservation.

- **PaymentDate**: Date of the payment.

- **Amount**: Total payment amount.

- **PaymentMethod**: Method used (e.g., credit card, PayPal).

- **PaymentStatus**: Status (e.g., Completed, Pending, Failed).

Constructing the Hospitality and Travel Conceptual Model

The conceptual model for the hospitality and travel industry integrates customer data, booking details, hotel and flight information, and payment processing. Core relationships include:

- **Customer-Reservation Relationship**: Each customer can have multiple reservations, forming a one-to-many (1:M) relationship.

- **Reservation-Hotel/Flight Relationship**: Reservations may be linked to hotels or flights, creating a many-to-one (M:1) relationship with each reservation tied to a specific service type.

- **Reservation-Payment Relationship**: Each reservation may have multiple payments, forming a one-to-many (1:M) relationship, which allows for partial payments or installments.

This model supports the management of customer interactions, reservation scheduling, and payment tracking.

Subject Areas: Customer Management, Booking Systems, Payment Processing

1. Customer Management

Handles customer information, preferences, and loyalty details to personalize service offerings.

- **Entities**: Customers, Reservations.

- **Primary Relationships**: Customer to Reservation (1:M).

- **Attributes**: Customer preferences, contact information, loyalty points.

2. Booking Systems

Manages hotel and flight reservations, including details on availability, booking status, and check-in/check-out.

- **Entities**: Reservations, Hotels, Flights.

- **Primary Relationships**: Reservation to Hotel (M:1), Reservation to Flight (M:1).

- **Attributes**: Service type, booking dates, reservation status.

3. Payment Processing

Tracks payments for reservations, including methods, amounts, and statuses.

- **Entities**: Payments, Reservations.

- **Primary Relationships**: Reservation to Payment (1:M).

- **Attributes**: Payment method, amount, status.

Cardinality and Relationship Analysis in Hospitality Models

Key relationships in the hospitality and travel data model help connect customers to their bookings and handle payment tracking:

- **Customer to Reservations**: Each customer can make multiple reservations, leading to a one-to-many (1:M) relationship.

- **Reservation to Hotels/Flights**: A reservation can link to either a hotel or flight, creating a many-to-one (M:1) relationship based on the service type.

- **Reservation to Payments**: Each reservation may have several payments, allowing for flexibility in payment plans and forming a one-to-many (1:M) relationship.

These relationships ensure accurate data representation of bookings, payments, and customer interactions.

Logical Data Model for Hospitality and Travel

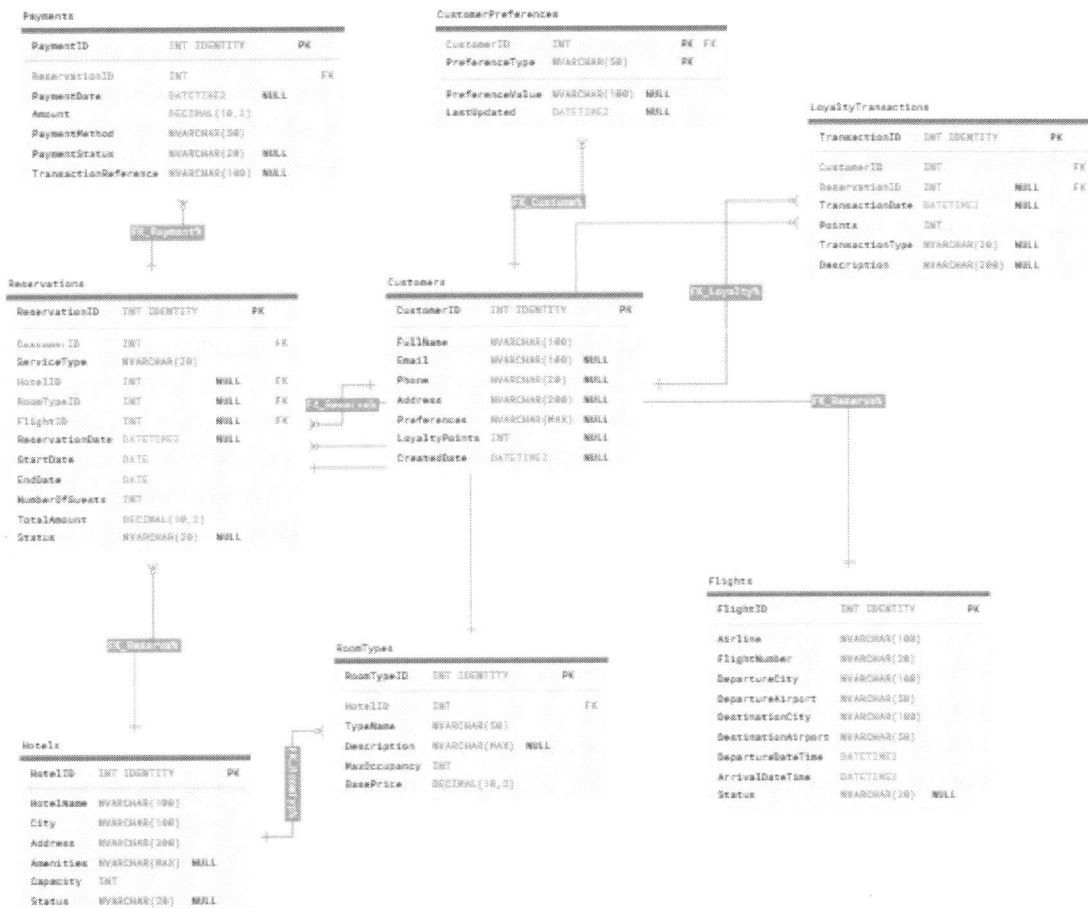

DDL for Model for Hospitality and Travel

```
-- Create Customers table
CREATE TABLE Customers (
    CustomerID INT PRIMARY KEY IDENTITY(1,1),
    FullName NVARCHAR(100) NOT NULL,
    Email NVARCHAR(100),
    Phone NVARCHAR(20),
    Address NVARCHAR(200),
    Preferences NVARCHAR(MAX),
    LoyaltyPoints INT DEFAULT 0,
    CreatedDate DATETIME2 DEFAULT GETDATE(),
    CONSTRAINT UC_Customer_Email UNIQUE (Email)
);

-- Create Hotels table
CREATE TABLE Hotels (
    HotelID INT PRIMARY KEY IDENTITY(1,1),
    HotelName NVARCHAR(100) NOT NULL,
    City NVARCHAR(100) NOT NULL,
    Address NVARCHAR(200) NOT NULL,
    Amenities NVARCHAR(MAX),
    Capacity INT NOT NULL,
    Status NVARCHAR(20) DEFAULT 'Active' CHECK (Status IN ('Active', 'Inactive', 'Under Maintenance')),
    CONSTRAINT UC_Hotel_Name_City UNIQUE (HotelName, City)
);

-- Create Room Types table
CREATE TABLE RoomTypes (
```

```
RoomTypeID INT PRIMARY KEY IDENTITY(1,1),

HotelID INT NOT NULL,

TypeName NVARCHAR(50) NOT NULL,

Description NVARCHAR(MAX),

MaxOccupancy INT NOT NULL,

BasePrice DECIMAL(10,2) NOT NULL,

CONSTRAINT FK_RoomTypes_Hotel FOREIGN KEY (HotelID)

    REFERENCES Hotels(HotelID)
);


-- Create Flights table
CREATE TABLE Flights (

    FlightID INT PRIMARY KEY IDENTITY(1,1),

    Airline NVARCHAR(100) NOT NULL,

    FlightNumber NVARCHAR(20) NOT NULL,

    DepartureCity NVARCHAR(100) NOT NULL,

    DepartureAirport NVARCHAR(50) NOT NULL,

    DestinationCity NVARCHAR(100) NOT NULL,

    DestinationAirport NVARCHAR(50) NOT NULL,

    DepartureDateTime DATETIME2 NOT NULL,

    ArrivalDateTime DATETIME2 NOT NULL,

    Status NVARCHAR(20) DEFAULT 'Scheduled'

        CHECK (Status IN ('Scheduled', 'Delayed', 'Cancelled', 'Completed')),

    CONSTRAINT UC_Flight_Number_DateTime UNIQUE (FlightNumber, DepartureDateTime)
);


-- Create Reservations table
CREATE TABLE Reservations (

    ReservationID INT PRIMARY KEY IDENTITY(1,1),

    CustomerID INT NOT NULL,
```

```sql
    ServiceType NVARCHAR(20) NOT NULL CHECK (ServiceType IN ('Hotel', 'Flight')),

    HotelID INT,

    RoomTypeID INT,

    FlightID INT,

    ReservationDate DATETIME2 DEFAULT GETDATE(),

    StartDate DATE NOT NULL,

    EndDate DATE NOT NULL,

    NumberOfGuests INT NOT NULL,

    TotalAmount DECIMAL(10,2) NOT NULL,

    Status NVARCHAR(20) DEFAULT 'Pending'

        CHECK (Status IN ('Pending', 'Confirmed', 'Cancelled', 'Completed')),

    CONSTRAINT FK_Reservations_Customer FOREIGN KEY (CustomerID)

        REFERENCES Customers(CustomerID),

    CONSTRAINT FK_Reservations_Hotel FOREIGN KEY (HotelID)

        REFERENCES Hotels(HotelID),

    CONSTRAINT FK_Reservations_RoomType FOREIGN KEY (RoomTypeID)

        REFERENCES RoomTypes(RoomTypeID),

    CONSTRAINT FK_Reservations_Flight FOREIGN KEY (FlightID)

        REFERENCES Flights(FlightID),

    CONSTRAINT CHK_Hotel_or_Flight CHECK (

        (ServiceType = 'Hotel' AND HotelID IS NOT NULL AND RoomTypeID IS NOT NULL AND FlightID IS NULL) OR

        (ServiceType = 'Flight' AND FlightID IS NOT NULL AND HotelID IS NULL AND RoomTypeID IS NULL)

    )

);


-- Create Payments table
CREATE TABLE Payments (

    PaymentID INT PRIMARY KEY IDENTITY(1,1),

    ReservationID INT NOT NULL,
```

```
PaymentDate DATETIME2 DEFAULT GETDATE(),

Amount DECIMAL(10,2) NOT NULL,

PaymentMethod NVARCHAR(50) NOT NULL,

PaymentStatus NVARCHAR(20) DEFAULT 'Pending'

    CHECK (PaymentStatus IN ('Pending', 'Completed', 'Failed', 'Refunded')),

TransactionReference NVARCHAR(100),

CONSTRAINT FK_Payments_Reservation FOREIGN KEY (ReservationID)

    REFERENCES Reservations(ReservationID)

);


-- Create CustomerPreferences bridge table (for detailed preference tracking)

CREATE TABLE CustomerPreferences (

    CustomerID INT,

    PreferenceType NVARCHAR(50),

    PreferenceValue NVARCHAR(100),

    LastUpdated DATETIME2 DEFAULT GETDATE(),

    CONSTRAINT PK_CustomerPreferences PRIMARY KEY (CustomerID, PreferenceType),

    CONSTRAINT FK_CustomerPreferences_Customer FOREIGN KEY (CustomerID)

        REFERENCES Customers(CustomerID)

);


-- Create LoyaltyTransactions table (for tracking point earnings and redemptions)

CREATE TABLE LoyaltyTransactions (

    TransactionID INT PRIMARY KEY IDENTITY(1,1),

    CustomerID INT NOT NULL,

    ReservationID INT,

    TransactionDate DATETIME2 DEFAULT GETDATE(),

    Points INT NOT NULL,

    TransactionType NVARCHAR(20) CHECK (TransactionType IN ('Earned', 'Redeemed')),

    Description NVARCHAR(200),
```

```
    CONSTRAINT FK_LoyaltyTransactions_Customer FOREIGN KEY (CustomerID)

        REFERENCES Customers(CustomerID),

    CONSTRAINT FK_LoyaltyTransactions_Reservation FOREIGN KEY (ReservationID)

        REFERENCES Reservations(ReservationID)

);


-- Create indexes for better query performance

CREATE INDEX IX_Reservations_Status ON Reservations(Status);

CREATE INDEX IX_Reservations_Dates ON Reservations(StartDate, EndDate);

CREATE INDEX IX_Payments_Status ON Payments(PaymentStatus);

CREATE INDEX IX_Flights_Status ON Flights(Status);

CREATE INDEX IX_Hotels_Status ON Hotels(Status);

CREATE INDEX IX_Customers_LoyaltyPoints ON Customers(LoyaltyPoints);
```

Exercise: Modeling Reservation-Customer Relationships

In this exercise, you'll create a model that includes customers, reservations, and payment data. Follow these steps:

1. **Define Entities**: Identify primary entities—Customers, Reservations, Payments.

2. **Establish Keys and Attributes**: Define primary keys, foreign keys, and relevant attributes for each entity.

3. **Create Relationships**: Model the relationships, focusing on cardinality for Customer-Reservation and Reservation-Payment.

Case Study: Data Model for a Hotel Booking System

In this case study, we explore a data model designed for a hotel booking system that manages customer bookings, tracks room availability, and processes payments:

1. **Customer Data**: Maintains details on customers, including contact information, loyalty points, and preferences.

2. **Room Reservations**: Handles room bookings for hotels, including check-in and check-out dates, room types, and booking status.

3. **Payment Processing**: Manages payments linked to room reservations, with support for multiple payment options and statuses.

This data model supports efficient booking management, enhances the customer experience by personalizing offerings, and ensures secure, reliable payment tracking.

Chapter Summary and Quiz

This chapter covered data modeling for the hospitality and travel industry, focusing on entities such as customers, reservations, hotels, flights, and payments. The data model ensures efficient booking management, enables smooth payment processing, and supports personalized services.

Quiz:

1. List three key entities in a hospitality and travel data model.

2. What relationship exists between Customers and Reservations?

3. How does the data model handle multiple payments for a single reservation?

4. Why is it important to model customer preferences in the hospitality industry?

A well-structured data model enables hospitality businesses to enhance customer experiences, streamline bookings, and manage payments effectively.

Chapter 15: Data Modeling for Real Estate and Property Management

Overview of Real Estate Data Needs: Property Listings, Rentals, and Transactions

The real estate and property management industry handles large amounts of data related to property listings, rental agreements, tenant information, ownership details, and financial transactions. Effective data models are essential for streamlining processes such as listing properties, managing leases, and tracking payments. Real estate models also facilitate operational efficiency, tenant and owner interactions, and compliance with legal requirements.

This chapter provides a comprehensive approach to data modeling for real estate, covering essential entities and relationships and exploring best practices for property and tenant management.

Key Entities: Properties, Tenants, Owners, Leases, Transactions

In real estate, certain core entities and their associated attributes are critical for modeling property management and transactional data:

1. **Properties**

   Represents the various properties managed, whether for sale, lease, or rental.

   - **PropertyID** (Primary Key): Unique identifier for each property.

   - **Address**: Property address, including street, city, state, and postal code.

   - **PropertyType**: Type of property (e.g., Residential, Commercial).

   - **Size**: Size of the property, often in square feet or meters.

   - **Amenities**: Available amenities (e.g., parking, gym, pool).

   - **OwnerID** (Foreign Key): Links to the owner of the property.

2. **Tenants**

   Represents individuals or organizations leasing a property.

Michael E. Kirshteyn, Ph.D

151

- **TenantID** (Primary Key): Unique identifier for each tenant.

- **FullName**: Full name of the tenant.

- **ContactInfo**: Tenant's contact details, including phone and email.

- **RentalHistory**: Record of previous properties rented.

- **LeaseID** (Foreign Key): Links to the current lease agreement, if applicable.

3. Owners

Represents the individuals or entities that own properties.

- **OwnerID** (Primary Key): Unique identifier for each owner.

- **FullName**: Name of the property owner.

- **ContactInfo**: Owner's contact details.

- **PortfolioValue**: Total value of properties owned.

- **OwnerType**: Type of owner (e.g., individual, corporate entity).

4. Leases

Contains information on lease agreements between tenants and property owners.

- **LeaseID** (Primary Key): Unique identifier for each lease.

- **PropertyID** (Foreign Key): Links to the leased property.

- **TenantID** (Foreign Key): Links to the tenant leasing the property.

- **StartDate**: Start date of the lease.

- **EndDate**: End date of the lease.

- **LeaseTerms**: Terms and conditions of the lease agreement.

- **RentAmount**: Monthly or annual rent amount.

5. Transactions

Manages payments and financial transactions related to lease agreements.

- **TransactionID** (Primary Key): Unique identifier for each transaction.

- **LeaseID** (Foreign Key): Links to the relevant lease.

- **PaymentDate**: Date of the payment.

- **Amount**: Amount paid in the transaction.

- **PaymentMethod**: Method of payment (e.g., credit card, bank transfer).

- **TransactionStatus**: Status of the transaction (e.g., Completed, Pending).

Building the Real Estate Conceptual Model

A well-designed conceptual model for real estate and property management connects tenants, property listings, leases, and financial transactions. Core relationships include:

- **Property-Tenant Relationship**: Properties are associated with tenants through lease agreements.

- **Owner-Property Relationship**: Each property has one or more owners, forming a one-to-many (1:M) relationship.

- **Lease-Transaction Relationship**: Each lease agreement may have multiple transactions, forming a one-to-many (1:M) relationship.

This model enables effective management of property listings, tenant information, and lease tracking, ensuring accurate and organized data representation.

Subject Areas: Property Listings, Tenant Management, Lease Tracking

1. **Property Listings**

   Manages data on available properties, including their attributes, ownership details, and statuses.

   - **Entities**: Properties, Owners.
   - **Primary Relationships**: Owner to Property (1:M).

- **Attributes**: Property details, amenities, owner information.

2. Tenant Management

Tracks tenant details, lease agreements, and rental history.

- **Entities**: Tenants, Leases.

- **Primary Relationships**: Tenant to Lease (1:1 or 1:M).

- **Attributes**: Tenant information, lease status, rental history.

3. Lease Tracking

Manages leases, payments, and terms for tenants and owners.

- **Entities**: Leases, Transactions.

- **Primary Relationships**: Lease to Transaction (1:M), Lease to Property (1:1).

- **Attributes**: Lease duration, payment terms, transaction history.

Cardinality and Relationships in Real Estate Models

The relationships in real estate data modeling reflect the connections between tenants, properties, leases, and payments:

- **Owner to Property**: An owner may have multiple properties, forming a one-to-many (1:M) relationship.

- **Property to Lease**: Each property can be leased multiple times, creating a one-to-many (1:M) relationship over time.

- **Lease to Transaction**: Multiple transactions are associated with a single lease, forming a one-to-many (1:M) relationship.

These relationships facilitate seamless property management and tenant interactions by capturing essential data flow.

Logical Data Model for Real Estate and Property Management

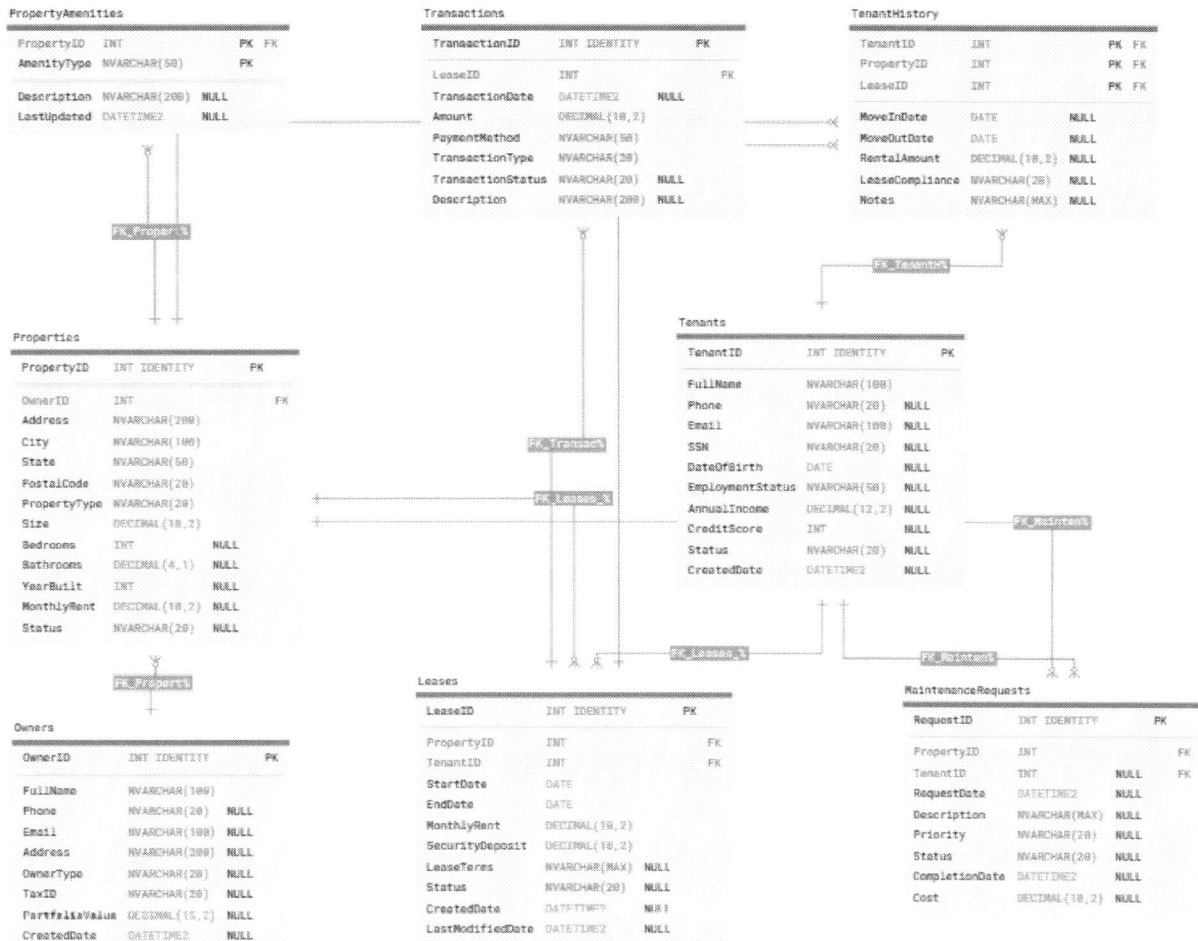

DDL for Real Estate and Property Management

-- Create Owners table

CREATE TABLE Owners (

    OwnerID INT PRIMARY KEY IDENTITY(1,1),

    FullName NVARCHAR(100) NOT NULL,

    Phone NVARCHAR(20),

    Email NVARCHAR(100),

    Address NVARCHAR(200),

```sql
    OwnerType NVARCHAR(20) CHECK (OwnerType IN ('Individual', 'Corporate', 'Trust')),

    TaxID NVARCHAR(20),

    PortfolioValue DECIMAL(15,2) DEFAULT 0,

    CreatedDate DATETIME2 DEFAULT GETDATE(),

    CONSTRAINT UC_Owner_Email UNIQUE (Email),

    CONSTRAINT UC_Owner_TaxID UNIQUE (TaxID)
);


-- Create Properties table
CREATE TABLE Properties (

    PropertyID INT PRIMARY KEY IDENTITY(1,1),

    OwnerID INT NOT NULL,

    Address NVARCHAR(200) NOT NULL,

    City NVARCHAR(100) NOT NULL,

    State NVARCHAR(50) NOT NULL,

    PostalCode NVARCHAR(20) NOT NULL,

    PropertyType NVARCHAR(20) NOT NULL

        CHECK (PropertyType IN ('Residential', 'Commercial', 'Industrial', 'Land')),

    Size DECIMAL(10,2) NOT NULL,

    Bedrooms INT,

    Bathrooms DECIMAL(4,1),

    YearBuilt INT,

    MonthlyRent DECIMAL(10,2),

    Status NVARCHAR(20) DEFAULT 'Available'

        CHECK (Status IN ('Available', 'Leased', 'Under Maintenance', 'Off Market')),

    CONSTRAINT FK_Properties_Owner FOREIGN KEY (OwnerID)

        REFERENCES Owners(OwnerID)
);


-- Create PropertyAmenities bridge table
```

```
CREATE TABLE PropertyAmenities (

    PropertyID INT,

    AmenityType NVARCHAR(50),

    Description NVARCHAR(200),

    LastUpdated DATETIME2 DEFAULT GETDATE(),

    CONSTRAINT PK_PropertyAmenities PRIMARY KEY (PropertyID, AmenityType),

    CONSTRAINT FK_PropertyAmenities_Property FOREIGN KEY (PropertyID)

        REFERENCES Properties(PropertyID)

);


-- Create Tenants table
CREATE TABLE Tenants (

    TenantID INT PRIMARY KEY IDENTITY(1,1),

    FullName NVARCHAR(100) NOT NULL,

    Phone NVARCHAR(20),

    Email NVARCHAR(100),

    SSN NVARCHAR(20),

    DateOfBirth DATE,

    EmploymentStatus NVARCHAR(50),

    AnnualIncome DECIMAL(12,2),

    CreditScore INT,

    Status NVARCHAR(20) DEFAULT 'Active'

        CHECK (Status IN ('Active', 'Inactive', 'Blacklisted')),

    CreatedDate DATETIME2 DEFAULT GETDATE(),

    CONSTRAINT UC_Tenant_Email UNIQUE (Email),

    CONSTRAINT UC_Tenant_SSN UNIQUE (SSN)

);


-- Create Leases table
CREATE TABLE Leases (
```

```
    LeaseID INT PRIMARY KEY IDENTITY(1,1),

    PropertyID INT NOT NULL,

    TenantID INT NOT NULL,

    StartDate DATE NOT NULL,

    EndDate DATE NOT NULL,

    MonthlyRent DECIMAL(10,2) NOT NULL,

    SecurityDeposit DECIMAL(10,2) NOT NULL,

    LeaseTerms NVARCHAR(MAX),

    Status NVARCHAR(20) DEFAULT 'Pending'
        CHECK (Status IN ('Pending', 'Active', 'Terminated', 'Expired')),

    CreatedDate DATETIME2 DEFAULT GETDATE(),

    LastModifiedDate DATETIME2 DEFAULT GETDATE(),

    CONSTRAINT FK_Leases_Property FOREIGN KEY (PropertyID)
        REFERENCES Properties(PropertyID),

    CONSTRAINT FK_Leases_Tenant FOREIGN KEY (TenantID)
        REFERENCES Tenants(TenantID),

    CONSTRAINT CHK_Lease_Dates CHECK (EndDate > StartDate)
);


-- Create Transactions table
CREATE TABLE Transactions (

    TransactionID INT PRIMARY KEY IDENTITY(1,1),

    LeaseID INT NOT NULL,

    TransactionDate DATETIME2 DEFAULT GETDATE(),

    Amount DECIMAL(10,2) NOT NULL,

    PaymentMethod NVARCHAR(50) NOT NULL,

    TransactionType NVARCHAR(20) NOT NULL
        CHECK (TransactionType IN ('Rent', 'Deposit', 'Fee', 'Refund')),

    TransactionStatus NVARCHAR(20) DEFAULT 'Pending'
        CHECK (TransactionStatus IN ('Pending', 'Completed', 'Failed', 'Refunded')),
```

```
    Description NVARCHAR(200),

    CONSTRAINT FK_Transactions_Lease FOREIGN KEY (LeaseID)

        REFERENCES Leases(LeaseID)

);


-- Create TenantHistory bridge table
CREATE TABLE TenantHistory (

    TenantID INT,

    PropertyID INT,

    LeaseID INT,

    MoveInDate DATE,

    MoveOutDate DATE,

    RentalAmount DECIMAL(10,2),

    LeaseCompliance NVARCHAR(20) DEFAULT 'Good'

        CHECK (LeaseCompliance IN ('Good', 'Fair', 'Poor')),

    Notes NVARCHAR(MAX),

    CONSTRAINT PK_TenantHistory PRIMARY KEY (TenantID, PropertyID, LeaseID),

    CONSTRAINT FK_TenantHistory_Tenant FOREIGN KEY (TenantID)

        REFERENCES Tenants(TenantID),

    CONSTRAINT FK_TenantHistory_Property FOREIGN KEY (PropertyID)

        REFERENCES Properties(PropertyID),

    CONSTRAINT FK_TenantHistory_Lease FOREIGN KEY (LeaseID)

        REFERENCES Leases(LeaseID)

);


-- Create MaintenanceRequests table
CREATE TABLE MaintenanceRequests (

    RequestID INT PRIMARY KEY IDENTITY(1,1),

    PropertyID INT NOT NULL,

    TenantID INT,
```

RequestDate DATETIME2 DEFAULT GETDATE(),

Description NVARCHAR(MAX),

Priority NVARCHAR(20) CHECK (Priority IN ('Low', 'Medium', 'High', 'Emergency')),

Status NVARCHAR(20) DEFAULT 'Pending'

   CHECK (Status IN ('Pending', 'In Progress', 'Completed', 'Cancelled')),

CompletionDate DATETIME2,

Cost DECIMAL(10,2),

CONSTRAINT FK_MaintenanceRequests_Property FOREIGN KEY (PropertyID)

   REFERENCES Properties(PropertyID),

CONSTRAINT FK_MaintenanceRequests_Tenant FOREIGN KEY (TenantID)

   REFERENCES Tenants(TenantID)

);

-- Create indexes for better query performance

CREATE INDEX IX_Properties_Status ON Properties(Status);

CREATE INDEX IX_Properties_Type ON Properties(PropertyType);

CREATE INDEX IX_Leases_Dates ON Leases(StartDate, EndDate);

CREATE INDEX IX_Leases_Status ON Leases(Status);

CREATE INDEX IX_Transactions_Date ON Transactions(TransactionDate);

CREATE INDEX IX_Transactions_Status ON Transactions(TransactionStatus);

CREATE INDEX IX_MaintenanceRequests_Status ON MaintenanceRequests(Status);

Exercise: Modeling Property-Tenant Relationships

In this exercise, you'll create a model for tracking property, tenant, and lease relationships. Follow these steps:

1. **Define Entities**: Identify key entities—Properties, Tenants, Leases.

2. **Establish Keys and Attributes**: Define primary and foreign keys, and list relevant attributes.

3. **Create Relationships**: Model relationships between entities, focusing on cardinality.

Case Study: Data Model for a Property Management Company

This case study involves designing a data model for a property management company that oversees property listings, leases, and tenant payments:

1. **Property Listings**: Contains information on available properties, including their sizes, types, and amenities.

2. **Tenant Information**: Tracks tenant details, preferences, and contact information.

3. **Lease Agreements**: Manages lease durations, rent amounts, and payment schedules.

4. **Transaction Processing**: Monitors rental payments and tracks transaction statuses.

This data model supports efficient property management, streamlined tenant onboarding, and organized lease and transaction tracking.

Chapter Summary and Quiz

In this chapter, we covered data modeling for the real estate and property management industry. We reviewed key entities such as Properties, Tenants, Leases, and Transactions, and examined how relationships support the management of listings, tenant records, and financial transactions.

Quiz:

1. What is the primary relationship between Owners and Properties?

2. List three key attributes for the Lease entity.

3. How are Transactions linked to Leases?

4. Why is it important to track tenant rental history?

By establishing clear relationships and cardinality in real estate data models, property managers can efficiently handle rentals, manage tenants, and process payments with greater accuracy.

Chapter 16: Data Modeling for Agriculture

Industry Overview: Farm Management, Crop Data, and Supply Chain

The agriculture industry increasingly relies on data to optimize farm management, track crop growth, manage resources, and ensure efficient supply chains. Agriculture data encompasses a range of information on crops, livestock, equipment, land use, environmental factors, and workforce management. As the industry adapts to modern technology, structured data models are essential for effective decision-making, resource allocation, and productivity tracking.

This chapter explores the fundamentals of data modeling for agriculture, covering the industry's essential entities, relationships, and best practices for structuring data for farming operations.

Key Entities: Farms, Crops, Equipment, Workers, Harvests

The primary entities in an agricultural data model capture core aspects of farming and resource management. Here are the key entities and attributes for an effective model:

1. Farms

Represents individual farms within an agricultural organization.

- **FarmID** (Primary Key): Unique identifier for each farm.

- **Location**: Geographical location of the farm, including latitude and longitude.

- **FarmSize**: Total area of the farm in acres or hectares.

- **FarmType**: Type of farm (e.g., Crop, Livestock, Mixed).

- **OwnerID** (Foreign Key): Links to the owner or organization managing the farm.

2. Crops

Represents different types of crops grown on farms.

- **CropID** (Primary Key): Unique identifier for each crop type.

- **CropType**: Type of crop (e.g., Corn, Wheat, Soy).

- **GrowthCycle**: Average growth duration from planting to harvest.

- **Season**: Preferred growing season(s) for the crop.

- **FarmID** (Foreign Key): Links the crop to the specific farm.

3. Equipment

Manages details of machinery and tools used on the farm.

- **EquipmentID** (Primary Key): Unique identifier for each piece of equipment.

- **EquipmentType**: Type of equipment (e.g., Tractor, Harvester).

- **MaintenanceSchedule**: Schedule for regular maintenance.

- **FarmID** (Foreign Key): Links equipment to the farm it's assigned to.

4. Workers

Represents individuals employed on the farm for crop or livestock management.

- **WorkerID** (Primary Key): Unique identifier for each worker.

- **FullName**: Name of the worker.

- **Role**: Worker's role (e.g., Farmhand, Supervisor, Technician).

- **ContactInfo**: Worker's contact details.

- **FarmID** (Foreign Key): Links the worker to their assigned farm.

5. Harvests

Tracks each harvest cycle and production outcome.

- **HarvestID** (Primary Key): Unique identifier for each harvest.

- **CropID** (Foreign Key): Links to the crop type harvested.

- **Quantity**: Total amount of the crop harvested.

- **HarvestDate**: Date of harvest.

Michael E. Kirshteyn, Ph.D

- **QualityGrade**: Quality rating of the harvest (e.g., Grade A, B, C).

Constructing the Agriculture Conceptual Model

A conceptual data model for agriculture links farms, crops, equipment, workers, and harvest data to provide a holistic view of farm operations. Key relationships include:

- **Farm-Crop Relationship**: Farms manage various crops, forming a one-to-many (1:M) relationship.

- **Farm-Worker Relationship**: Each farm employs multiple workers, also forming a one-to-many (1:M) relationship.

- **Crop-Harvest Relationship**: Each crop can have multiple harvests, creating a one-to-many (1:M) relationship.

This model allows efficient tracking of resources, operations, and outcomes, facilitating better decision-making across farm management.

Subject Areas: Farm Management, Crop Tracking, Worker Management

1. Farm Management

Encompasses data related to farms, including equipment, resource allocation, and workforce.

- **Entities**: Farms, Equipment, Workers.
- **Primary Relationships**: Farm to Equipment (1:M), Farm to Worker (1:M).
- **Attributes**: Farm location, farm type, equipment details, worker roles.

2. Crop Tracking

Manages crop growth, maintenance schedules, and harvest tracking.

- **Entities**: Crops, Harvests.

- **Primary Relationships**: Crop to Harvest (1:M).

- **Attributes**: Crop type, growth cycle, quantity harvested, harvest quality.

3. Worker Management

Covers data on workers, their roles, and responsibilities on the farm.

- **Entities**: Workers, Farms.

- **Primary Relationships**: Farm to Worker (1:M).

- **Attributes**: Worker information, assigned farm, contact details, role.

Cardinality and Relationships in Agriculture Models

The relationships in agriculture data modeling include:

- **Farm to Crop**: A farm may cultivate multiple crops, creating a one-to-many (1:M) relationship.

- **Farm to Worker**: Each farm can employ multiple workers, forming a one-to-many (1:M) relationship.

- **Crop to Harvest**: Each crop may undergo several harvests, forming a one-to-many (1:M) relationship.

These relationships are essential for effective farm management, ensuring accurate tracking of operations, resource allocation, and productivity.

Data Modeling for Agriculture / Farm Management, Crop Data, and Supply Chain

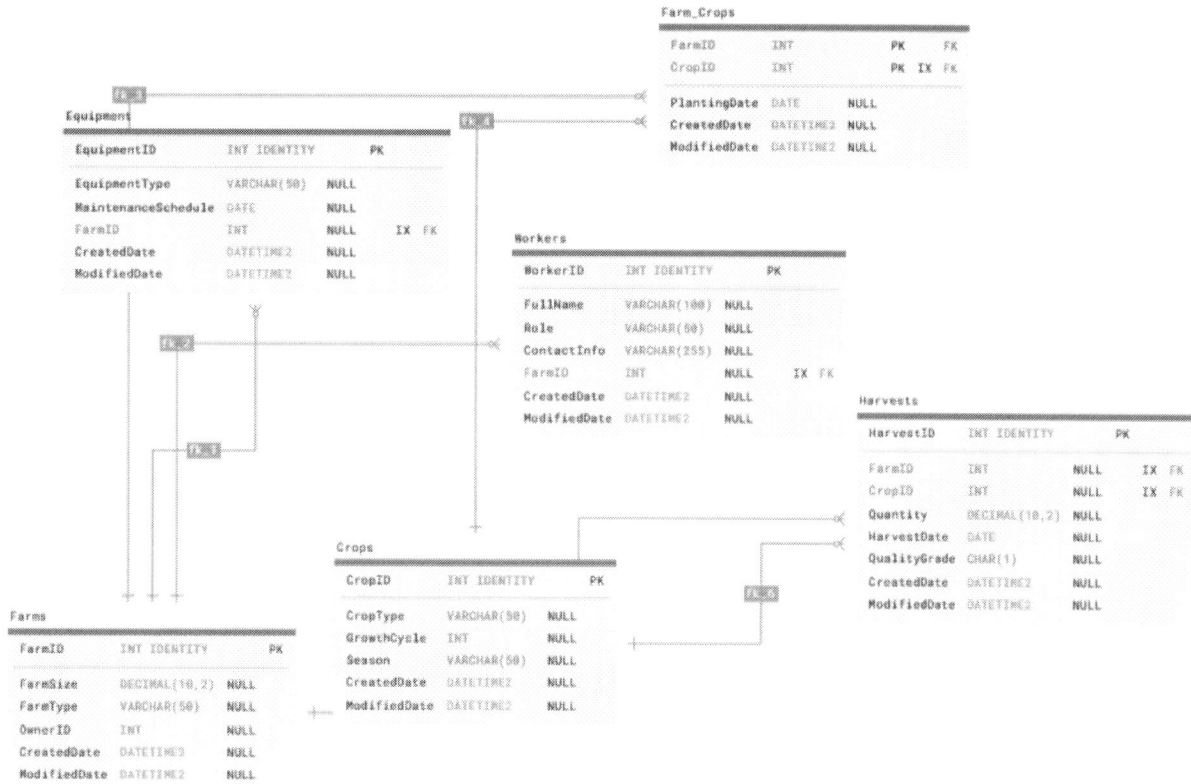

DDL for Agriculture / Farm Management, Crop Data, and Supply Chain

-- Create Farms table

CREATE TABLE Farms (

    FarmID INT PRIMARY KEY IDENTITY(1,1),

    Location GEOGRAPHY,

    FarmSize DECIMAL(10,2),

    FarmType VARCHAR(50) CHECK (FarmType IN ('Crop', 'Livestock', 'Mixed')),

    OwnerID INT,

    CreatedDate DATETIME2 DEFAULT GETDATE(),

    ModifiedDate DATETIME2 DEFAULT GETDATE()

);

```
-- Create Crops table
CREATE TABLE Crops (
    CropID INT PRIMARY KEY IDENTITY(1,1),
    CropType VARCHAR(50),
    GrowthCycle INT, -- Duration in days
    Season VARCHAR(50),
    CreatedDate DATETIME2 DEFAULT GETDATE(),
    ModifiedDate DATETIME2 DEFAULT GETDATE()
);


-- Create Equipment table
CREATE TABLE Equipment (
    EquipmentID INT PRIMARY KEY IDENTITY(1,1),
    EquipmentType VARCHAR(50),
    MaintenanceSchedule DATE,
    FarmID INT,
    CreatedDate DATETIME2 DEFAULT GETDATE(),
    ModifiedDate DATETIME2 DEFAULT GETDATE(),
    FOREIGN KEY (FarmID) REFERENCES Farms(FarmID)
);


-- Create Workers table
CREATE TABLE Workers (
    WorkerID INT PRIMARY KEY IDENTITY(1,1),
    FullName VARCHAR(100),
    Role VARCHAR(50),
    ContactInfo VARCHAR(255),
    FarmID INT,
    CreatedDate DATETIME2 DEFAULT GETDATE(),
    ModifiedDate DATETIME2 DEFAULT GETDATE(),
```

```
    FOREIGN KEY (FarmID) REFERENCES Farms(FarmID)
);


-- Create Farm_Crops bridge table for the many-to-many relationship between Farms and Crops
CREATE TABLE Farm_Crops (
    FarmID INT,
    CropID INT,
    PlantingDate DATE,
    CreatedDate DATETIME2 DEFAULT GETDATE(),
    ModifiedDate DATETIME2 DEFAULT GETDATE(),
    PRIMARY KEY (FarmID, CropID),
    FOREIGN KEY (FarmID) REFERENCES Farms(FarmID),
    FOREIGN KEY (CropID) REFERENCES Crops(CropID)
);


-- Create Harvests table
CREATE TABLE Harvests (
    HarvestID INT PRIMARY KEY IDENTITY(1,1),
    FarmID INT,
    CropID INT,
    Quantity DECIMAL(10,2),
    HarvestDate DATE,
    QualityGrade CHAR(1) CHECK (QualityGrade IN ('A', 'B', 'C')),
    CreatedDate DATETIME2 DEFAULT GETDATE(),
    ModifiedDate DATETIME2 DEFAULT GETDATE(),
    FOREIGN KEY (FarmID) REFERENCES Farms(FarmID),
    FOREIGN KEY (CropID) REFERENCES Crops(CropID)
);


-- Create indexes for better query performance
```

```
CREATE INDEX IX_Equipment_FarmID ON Equipment(FarmID);

CREATE INDEX IX_Workers_FarmID ON Workers(FarmID);

CREATE INDEX IX_FarmCrops_CropID ON Farm_Crops(CropID);

CREATE INDEX IX_Harvests_FarmID_CropID ON Harvests(FarmID, CropID);


-- Create trigger to update ModifiedDate
CREATE TRIGGER TR_Farms_Update ON Farms

AFTER UPDATE AS

BEGIN

    UPDATE Farms

    SET ModifiedDate = GETDATE()

    FROM Farms f

    INNER JOIN inserted i ON f.FarmID = i.FarmID;

END;


-- Repeat similar triggers for other tables
CREATE TRIGGER TR_Crops_Update ON Crops

AFTER UPDATE AS

BEGIN

    UPDATE Crops

    SET ModifiedDate = GETDATE()

    FROM Crops c

    INNER JOIN inserted i ON c.CropID = i.CropID;

END;


-- Add more similar triggers for Equipment, Workers, Farm_Crops, and Harvests tables
```

Exercise: Modeling Farm-Crop and Worker-Crop Relationships

For this exercise, you will model the relationships between farms, crops, and workers. Follow these steps:

1. **Define Entities**: Identify the primary entities: Farms, Crops, Workers, and Harvests.

2. **Assign Keys and Attributes**: Define primary and foreign keys, and determine relevant attributes.

3. **Create Relationships**: Draw relationships, focusing on cardinality.

Case Study: Data Model for a Farm Management System

In this case study, we design a data model for a farm management system that supports tracking crops, equipment, workers, and harvests:

1. **Farm Management**: Tracks farm details, equipment, and workforce assignments.

2. **Crop Lifecycle**: Monitors the planting, growth, and harvest of crops on each farm.

3. **Worker Information**: Tracks workers assigned to farms, including roles and responsibilities.

4. **Harvest Tracking**: Records harvest outcomes, quality grades, and quantities for each crop.

This data model allows farm managers to make data-driven decisions on crop cycles, equipment needs, and workforce management, ultimately leading to more efficient and productive operations.

Chapter Summary and Quiz

In this chapter, we explored data modeling for the agriculture industry. We examined the key entities—Farms, Crops, Equipment, Workers, and Harvests—and looked at subject areas like Farm Management, Crop Tracking, and Worker Management. Understanding these relationships and cardinalities allows for effective farm management.

Quiz:

1. What is the relationship between Farms and Crops?

Michael E. Kirshteyn, Ph.D

2. List two key attributes for the Harvest entity.

3. How are Equipment and Farms linked in an agricultural data model?

4. Why is it important to track worker roles and assignments?

By designing an efficient data model, agriculture businesses can ensure better tracking of resources and productivity, optimizing each stage from planting to harvest.

Chapter 17: Data Modeling for Media and Entertainment

Overview of Data Needs in Media: Content, Consumers, Engagement, and Licensing

The media and entertainment industry is highly data-driven, relying on robust data models to handle content creation, distribution, consumer engagement, licensing, and monetization. With the rise of streaming platforms, social media, and digital content, media companies gather vast amounts of information on user preferences, content consumption, subscription patterns, and more. Efficient data models are critical for managing this data to enhance user experience, drive engagement, optimize licensing, and ensure data compliance.

This chapter provides an overview of data modeling tailored to the media and entertainment industry, focusing on the essential entities, subject areas, and relationships needed to support comprehensive data management.

Key Entities: Content, Users, Subscriptions, Ratings, Actors

Media and entertainment data models require specific entities that capture core aspects of content management and consumer interactions. Here are the key entities and their primary attributes:

1. **Content**

   Represents all types of media content available to users, including movies, shows, music, and more.

   - **ContentID** (Primary Key): Unique identifier for each piece of content.

   - **Title**: Title of the content.

   - **Type**: Type of content (e.g., Movie, Series, Song, Podcast).

   - **Genre**: Genre(s) associated with the content.

   - **ReleaseDate**: Date when the content was released.

   - **Duration**: Length of the content (e.g., runtime for videos, track length for audio).

   - **LicensingStatus**: Status of licensing rights (e.g., Active, Expired).

2. Users

Represents individuals who consume content on the platform.

- **UserID** (Primary Key): Unique identifier for each user.

- **Username**: User's chosen name on the platform.

- **SubscriptionType**: Type of subscription (e.g., Free, Premium).

- **RegistrationDate**: Date the user registered.

- **Email**: Contact email for the user.

3. Subscriptions

Tracks details about user subscriptions and payment plans.

- **SubscriptionID** (Primary Key): Unique identifier for each subscription record.

- **UserID** (Foreign Key): Links to the specific user.

- **SubscriptionPlan**: Type of plan (e.g., Monthly, Annual).

- **StartDate**: Start date of the subscription.

- **EndDate**: End date of the subscription.

- **Status**: Status of the subscription (e.g., Active, Canceled).

4. Ratings

Manages user ratings and feedback on content.

- **RatingID** (Primary Key): Unique identifier for each rating.

- **UserID** (Foreign Key): Links to the user who provided the rating.

- **ContentID** (Foreign Key): Links to the rated content.

- **RatingScore**: Numerical rating (e.g., 1-5 stars).

- **Review**: Text review given by the user.

- **RatingDate**: Date the rating was submitted.

5. Actors

Represents actors or artists associated with content, primarily relevant for video and music.

- **ActorID** (Primary Key): Unique identifier for each actor or artist.

- **Name**: Full name of the actor or artist.

- **DOB**: Date of birth.

- **ContentID** (Foreign Key): Links to the content they are associated with.

- **Role**: Role played by the actor or involvement type (e.g., Lead, Supporting, Director).

Constructing the Media Conceptual Model

The conceptual data model for media integrates content, users, subscriptions, and engagement metrics. The essential relationships include:

- **User-Content Relationship**: Users interact with various content, creating a many-to-many (M:N) relationship facilitated by the Ratings table.

- **User-Subscription Relationship**: Each user can have one or more subscriptions over time, forming a one-to-many (1:M) relationship.

- **Content-Actor Relationship**: Content may feature multiple actors, and each actor can be involved in multiple pieces of content, forming a many-to-many (M:N) relationship.

The media model captures the lifecycle of content management, user engagement, and licensing, helping companies optimize content recommendations and enhance the viewer experience.

Subject Areas: Content Management, User Engagement, Licensing

1. **Content Management**

Covers the organization, classification, and licensing of media content.

- **Entities**: Content, Actors.

- **Primary Relationships**: Content to Actor (M:N).

- **Attributes**: Content type, genre, duration, licensing status.

2. User Engagement

Manages user interaction with content, including ratings, views, and feedback.

- **Entities**: Users, Ratings.

- **Primary Relationships**: User to Content via Ratings (M:N).

- **Attributes**: User profile, rating score, review text, rating date.

3. Licensing

Tracks content licensing status and rights management.

- **Entities**: Content.

- **Primary Relationships**: Content licensing status and renewal schedule.

- **Attributes**: Licensing status, release date, genre, type.

Cardinality and Relationships in Media Models

The relationships central to the media data model include:

- **User to Content (via Ratings)**: Represents how users interact with content, a many-to-many (M:N) relationship.

- **User to Subscription**: Users can have multiple subscription records, creating a one-to-many (1:M) relationship.

- **Content to Actor**: Content often includes multiple actors, while actors may feature in multiple pieces of content, a many-to-many (M:N) relationship.

Understanding these relationships helps in designing databases that enable effective tracking of user engagement and content performance.

Logical Data Model for Media and Entertainment

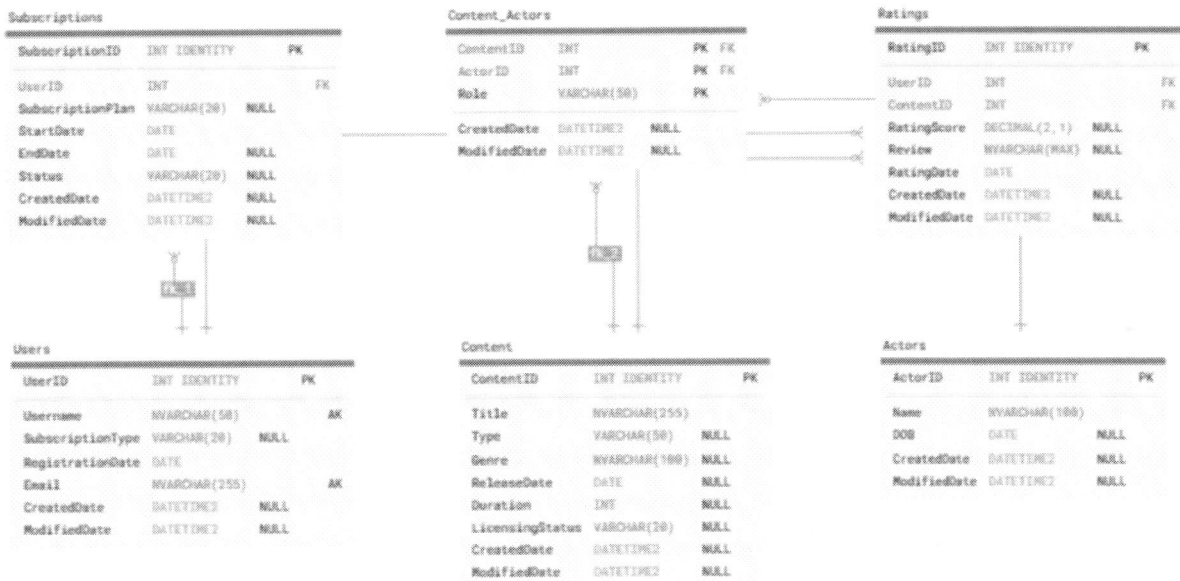

DDL for Media and Entertainment

-- Create Content table

CREATE TABLE Content (

    ContentID INT PRIMARY KEY IDENTITY(1,1),

    Title NVARCHAR(255) NOT NULL,

    Type VARCHAR(50) CHECK (Type IN ('Movie', 'Series', 'Song', 'Podcast')),

    Genre NVARCHAR(100),

    ReleaseDate DATE,

    Duration INT, -- Duration in minutes

    LicensingStatus VARCHAR(20) CHECK (LicensingStatus IN ('Active', 'Expired', 'Pending')),

Michael E. Kirshteyn, Ph.D

```
    CreatedDate DATETIME2 DEFAULT GETDATE(),

    ModifiedDate DATETIME2 DEFAULT GETDATE()

);


-- Create Users table

CREATE TABLE Users (

    UserID INT PRIMARY KEY IDENTITY(1,1),

    Username NVARCHAR(50) NOT NULL UNIQUE,

    SubscriptionType VARCHAR(20) CHECK (SubscriptionType IN ('Free', 'Premium')),

    RegistrationDate DATE NOT NULL,

    Email NVARCHAR(255) NOT NULL UNIQUE,

    CreatedDate DATETIME2 DEFAULT GETDATE(),

    ModifiedDate DATETIME2 DEFAULT GETDATE()

);


-- Create Subscriptions table

CREATE TABLE Subscriptions (

    SubscriptionID INT PRIMARY KEY IDENTITY(1,1),

    UserID INT NOT NULL,

    SubscriptionPlan VARCHAR(20) CHECK (SubscriptionPlan IN ('Monthly', 'Annual')),

    StartDate DATE NOT NULL,

    EndDate DATE,

    Status VARCHAR(20) CHECK (Status IN ('Active', 'Canceled', 'Expired')),

    CreatedDate DATETIME2 DEFAULT GETDATE(),

    ModifiedDate DATETIME2 DEFAULT GETDATE(),

    FOREIGN KEY (UserID) REFERENCES Users(UserID)

);


-- Create Actors table

CREATE TABLE Actors (
```

```
    ActorID INT PRIMARY KEY IDENTITY(1,1),

    Name NVARCHAR(100) NOT NULL,

    DOB DATE,

    CreatedDate DATETIME2 DEFAULT GETDATE(),

    ModifiedDate DATETIME2 DEFAULT GETDATE()
);


-- Create Content_Actors bridge table for the many-to-many relationship
CREATE TABLE Content_Actors (

    ContentID INT NOT NULL,

    ActorID INT NOT NULL,

    Role VARCHAR(50) CHECK (Role IN ('Lead', 'Supporting', 'Director', 'Producer')),

    CreatedDate DATETIME2 DEFAULT GETDATE(),

    ModifiedDate DATETIME2 DEFAULT GETDATE(),

    PRIMARY KEY (ContentID, ActorID, Role),

    FOREIGN KEY (ContentID) REFERENCES Content(ContentID),

    FOREIGN KEY (ActorID) REFERENCES Actors(ActorID)
);


-- Create Ratings table (serves as a bridge table between Users and Content)
CREATE TABLE Ratings (

    RatingID INT PRIMARY KEY IDENTITY(1,1),

    UserID INT NOT NULL,

    ContentID INT NOT NULL,

    RatingScore DECIMAL(2,1) CHECK (RatingScore >= 1 AND RatingScore <= 5),

    Review NVARCHAR(MAX),

    RatingDate DATE NOT NULL,

    CreatedDate DATETIME2 DEFAULT GETDATE(),

    ModifiedDate DATETIME2 DEFAULT GETDATE(),

    FOREIGN KEY (UserID) REFERENCES Users(UserID),
```

```
    FOREIGN KEY (ContentID) REFERENCES Content(ContentID)
);


-- Create indexes for better query performance
CREATE INDEX IX_Content_Title ON Content(Title);

CREATE INDEX IX_Content_Type_Genre ON Content(Type, Genre);

CREATE INDEX IX_Users_Email ON Users(Email);

CREATE INDEX IX_Subscriptions_UserID ON Subscriptions(UserID);

CREATE INDEX IX_Subscriptions_Status ON Subscriptions(Status);

CREATE INDEX IX_ContentActors_ActorID ON Content_Actors(ActorID);

CREATE INDEX IX_Ratings_ContentID ON Ratings(ContentID);

CREATE INDEX IX_Ratings_UserID ON Ratings(UserID);

CREATE INDEX IX_Ratings_Score ON Ratings(RatingScore);


-- Create triggers to maintain ModifiedDate
CREATE TRIGGER TR_Content_Update ON Content

AFTER UPDATE AS

BEGIN

   UPDATE Content

   SET ModifiedDate = GETDATE()

   FROM Content c

   INNER JOIN inserted i ON c.ContentID = i.ContentID;

END;


CREATE TRIGGER TR_Users_Update ON Users

AFTER UPDATE AS

BEGIN

   UPDATE Users

   SET ModifiedDate = GETDATE()

   FROM Users u
```

```
    INNER JOIN inserted i ON u.UserID = i.UserID;

END;


-- Add similar triggers for other tables


-- Create view for content performance analytics
CREATE VIEW vw_ContentPerformance AS
SELECT
    c.ContentID,
    c.Title,
    c.Type,
    c.Genre,
    COUNT(DISTINCT r.UserID) as TotalRatings,
    AVG(r.RatingScore) as AverageRating,
    COUNT(DISTINCT ca.ActorID) as ActorCount
FROM Content c
LEFT JOIN Ratings r ON c.ContentID = r.ContentID
LEFT JOIN Content_Actors ca ON c.ContentID = ca.ContentID
GROUP BY c.ContentID, c.Title, c.Type, c.Genre;
```

Exercise: Modeling User-Content Relationships

In this exercise, you will model the relationship between users and content using the Ratings entity. Follow these steps:

1. **Define Entities**: Identify the primary entities: Users, Content, and Ratings.

2. **Assign Keys and Attributes**: Define primary and foreign keys and list relevant attributes.

3. **Create Relationships**: Establish relationships, focusing on cardinality.

Case Study: Data Model for a Streaming Service

In this case study, we develop a data model for a streaming service that handles user subscriptions, content interactions, and recommendations.

1. **Content Library Management**: Tracks media content, genres, release dates, and actors.

2. **User Subscriptions**: Maintains user subscription status, plan details, and renewal dates.

3. **User Ratings**: Records user ratings and reviews, enabling personalized recommendations.

4. **Content Engagement Analytics**: Provides insights into popular content, user feedback, and engagement metrics.

This model supports a data-driven approach to delivering personalized recommendations, tracking content performance, and managing licensing, which is vital for competitive streaming services.

Chapter Summary and Quiz

This chapter introduced data modeling for the media and entertainment industry, focusing on entities like Content, Users, Subscriptions, Ratings, and Actors. We explored subject areas for managing content, user engagement, and licensing while analyzing key relationships and cardinality.

Quiz:

1. What is the relationship between Users and Content in terms of Ratings?

2. List three attributes for the Content entity.

3. Explain the significance of the User-Subscription relationship.

4. Why is the Content-Actor relationship a many-to-many relationship?

Data modeling for media and entertainment offers a foundation for optimized user experience, content management, and licensing efficiency. With effective data models, media companies can better engage users and manage their content libraries.

Chapter 18: Advanced Concepts in Logical Data Modeling

Introduction

In logical data modeling, advanced techniques can enhance data integrity, efficiency, and scalability. This chapter delves into key advanced concepts, including handling complex relationships, using composite and surrogate keys, applying normalization and denormalization, and implementing integrity constraints. Each topic builds upon foundational data modeling skills, enabling you to design more robust and flexible models.

Handling Complex Relationships and Cardinality

Complex relationships and cardinality types are essential to accurately represent real-world scenarios. These include many-to-many (M:N) relationships, recursive relationships, and identifying vs. non-identifying relationships.

- **Many-to-Many (M:N) Relationships**: When multiple records in one entity relate to multiple records in another, such as the User-Content relationship in a media application, an associative (or bridge) table is often needed.

- **Recursive Relationships**: Situations where an entity relates to itself, such as an Employee supervising another Employee. Recursive relationships are common in hierarchical structures.

- **Identifying and Non-Identifying Relationships**: An identifying relationship occurs when the child entity depends on the parent's existence, often requiring a composite primary key. Non-identifying relationships allow each entity to be independently referenced.

-**Outriggers**: In logical database modeling, *outriggers* are tables used to represent hierarchical relationships without requiring self-joins. An outrigger table stores related data that would otherwise require a self-join to represent hierarchical structures, such as parent-child relationships, in a more efficient and maintainable way. Instead of joining a table to itself, outriggers allow a modeler to create a separate table that links to the main entity, simplifying queries and improving performance.

Using Composite and Surrogate Keys in Models

Keys are crucial for uniquely identifying records. This section covers scenarios that benefit from composite and surrogate keys.

- **Composite Keys**: These are made from two or more attributes that together uniquely identify a record. Composite keys are useful in associative entities, where no single attribute can uniquely identify a record (e.g., `UserID` and `ContentID` together in a Ratings entity).

- **Surrogate Keys**: A surrogate key is a unique identifier that has no meaning outside the database context, such as an auto-incremented integer. Surrogate keys are ideal when natural keys are complex, change frequently, or are composite, simplifying data joins and index management.

Normalization and Denormalization Best Practices

Normalization organizes data to reduce redundancy and improve integrity, while denormalization reintroduces redundancy for performance gains in specific scenarios.

1. **Normalization**:

   - **1NF (First Normal Form)**: Ensure all attribute values are atomic.

   - **2NF (Second Normal Form)**: Achieve 1NF and remove partial dependencies by ensuring non-key attributes depend on the entire primary key.

   - **3NF (Third Normal Form)**: Achieve 2NF and remove transitive dependencies, where non-key attributes should not depend on other non-key attributes.

2. **Denormalization**:

   - **Benefits**: Denormalization improves performance, especially in read-heavy systems where complex joins slow down queries.

   - **Drawbacks**: Increases data redundancy, storage requirements, and potential data inconsistencies.

   Use Case: A denormalized structure might combine `Customer`, `Orders`, and `Products` into a single entity in an e-commerce database for faster reporting.

Understanding Data Integrity and Referential Integrity Constraints

Data integrity ensures data accuracy and consistency, while referential integrity maintains valid linkages between related entities.

- **Data Integrity Constraints**:

  - **Domain Constraints**: Ensure attributes fall within valid ranges or categories.

  - **Uniqueness Constraints**: Guarantee that values are unique across a given attribute or combination of attributes.

  - **Check Constraints**: Apply logical conditions that attribute values must satisfy, such as a non-negative constraint on quantities.

- **Referential Integrity Constraints**:

  - **Primary and Foreign Key Relationships**: Define and enforce dependencies between entities.

  - **Cascading Updates and Deletes**: Specify what happens to related records when the parent record is updated or deleted (e.g., cascading deletes to remove dependent child records automatically).

Hands-On Exercises: Applying Advanced Techniques to Previous Models

1. **Exercise 1**: Update the Media Data Model with a Surrogate Key for `Content` and apply a recursive relationship for `Series` within the same `Content` entity to capture multi-episode relationships.

2. **Exercise 2**: Normalize the Insurance Data Model to 3NF, identifying potential denormalization points for faster reporting. Add domain constraints to prevent negative premium amounts.

3. **Exercise 3**: Implement referential integrity constraints in the Education Data Model to enforce valid links between `Students`, `Courses`, and `Enrollments`. Apply cascading delete behavior in `Enrollments` to remove records when a `Student` is deleted.

4. **Exercise 4**: Define composite keys in the Transportation Data Model for managing `Route` and `Vehicle` entities in a many-to-many relationship. Use a bridge table with composite keys to handle this association.

Chapter Summary and Quiz

This chapter covered advanced concepts in logical data modeling, including complex relationships, composite and surrogate keys, normalization and denormalization practices, and data integrity constraints. Mastering these concepts enhances data model flexibility, efficiency, and accuracy.

Quiz:

1. What is the purpose of a surrogate key?

2. Describe a scenario where a recursive relationship is needed.

3. What is the difference between normalization and denormalization?

4. How does a cascading delete constraint work in referential integrity?

5. Why might you use a composite key in a bridge table for a many-to-many relationship?

With these advanced techniques, you can now refine and optimize data models, ensuring they are both robust and capable of handling complex real-world scenarios.

Appendices

- Appendix A: Glossary of Terms

1. Cardinality

The relationship between entities in a data model, indicating how many instances of one entity relate to instances of another. Common cardinalities include one-to-one, one-to-many, and many-to-many.

2. Conceptual Data Model

A high-level representation of the data requirements for a specific business domain, focused on defining the major entities, their relationships, and key attributes without concern for database-specific details.

3. Composite Key

A key formed by combining two or more columns in a table to uniquely identify a record. Used when no single attribute can serve as a unique identifier.

4. Data Decomposition

The process of breaking down a complex system or dataset into smaller, more manageable parts. In data modeling, this involves dividing data into logical components such as entities, attributes, and relationships.

5. Data Integrity

Ensuring the accuracy and consistency of data throughout its lifecycle. It involves constraints that prevent invalid data from entering the database.

6. Data Model

A visual representation of the structure of a database, including entities, attributes, and relationships. It serves as a blueprint for database design and development.

7. Denormalization

The process of adding redundancy to a database by combining tables or adding data that would otherwise be spread across multiple tables, aimed at improving read performance at the cost of write efficiency.

8. Entity

A distinct object or concept in the data model that represents a thing of interest. Examples include customer, product, or order.

9. Entity-Relationship Diagram (ERD)

A diagram that visually represents the entities within a system and their relationships to one another. ERDs are commonly used to design databases and illustrate data structures.

10. Identifying Relationship

A relationship between two entities in which the existence of one entity depends on the existence of another. The child entity's key includes the key of the parent entity.

11. Non-Identifying Relationship

A relationship between two entities where the existence of one entity does not depend on the other. The child entity does not inherit the parent entity's key as part of its primary key.

12. Normalization

The process of organizing a database to reduce redundancy and dependency by splitting large tables into smaller, more focused tables. The goal is to ensure that data is stored efficiently and without unnecessary duplication.

13. Primary Key

A field or a combination of fields in a database table that uniquely identifies each record in the table. It cannot contain null values and must be unique for each record.

14. Referential Integrity

A database constraint that ensures relationships between tables are consistent. Specifically, it ensures that a foreign key in one table matches a primary key in another table, or that foreign keys are null when appropriate.

15. Relationship

A logical connection between two or more entities in a data model. Relationships define how entities interact with one another and may have cardinalities (e.g., one-to-many, many-to-many).

16. Surrogate Key

An artificial key used to uniquely identify a record in a database. It is typically a numeric or alphanumeric identifier and does not have any real-world meaning.

17. Subject Area

A distinct portion of the data model that focuses on a specific business domain or function. Examples include "Customer Management," "Order Processing," or "Inventory Control."

18. Transactional Data

Data related to the transactions or actions that occur within a system, such as sales orders, purchases, or service requests. Transactional data typically records events in a time-sensitive context.

19. Unique Key

A constraint that ensures all values in a particular column or a set of columns in a database table are unique. Unlike primary keys, unique keys can accept null values.

20. Visualization

The graphical representation of data models, often using tools like ER diagrams or UML diagrams, to simplify understanding and communication of complex data structures and relationships.

21. Working Data Model

An evolving, practical version of a data model used for development and testing purposes. It is a more detailed version of a conceptual model, focusing on implementation details and often includes normalization and other optimizations.

22. Attribute

A characteristic or property of an entity. For example, an attribute of a "Customer" entity might be "Customer Name" or "Customer ID."

23. Foreign Key

A column or set of columns in one table that uniquely identifies a row in another table. It is used to create a link between two tables, establishing a relationship.

24. Data Constraints

Rules or restrictions placed on the data in a database to ensure accuracy and integrity. These include primary keys, foreign keys, uniqueness, and not null constraints.

25. Data Modeling

The process of creating a data model to represent the structure, relationships, and constraints of data within a system or database. It is a critical step in the database design and development lifecycle.

26. Schema

The structure of a database, including the tables, fields, relationships, and other elements. It defines the organization of data and how different pieces of data relate to one another.

27. Temporal Data

Data that involves time-based information, such as timestamps, dates, or durations, used to track the timing of events or transactions in a system.

28. Multivalued Attribute

An attribute that can hold multiple values for a single entity. For example, a "Phone Numbers" attribute might store multiple phone numbers for a single customer.

29. Data Dictionary

A collection of metadata that defines the structure, relationships, and constraints of a database. It provides detailed information about each element within the database schema.

30. Fact Table

A table in a data warehouse that stores quantitative data for analysis, typically containing metrics or measures, such as sales revenue or order count. Fact tables are often linked to dimension tables in star or snowflake schemas.

31. Dimension Table

A table in a data warehouse that provides context to the facts stored in the fact table. It typically contains descriptive information such as "Product," "Customer," or "Time."

This glossary serves as a guide to key terms used in data modeling throughout this book, offering clarity for readers as they engage with the more technical content and exercises in each chapter.

- Appendix B: References

1. **Batini, C., Ceri, S., & Navathe, S. B.** (2009). *Conceptual Design: An Evolutionary View*. Springer.

This book provides a comprehensive overview of conceptual data modeling techniques and offers insights into the evolution of data design methodologies.

2. **Harrington, J. L.** (2016). *Relational Database Design and Implementation* (4th ed.). Morgan Kaufmann.

A practical guide to database design, this book emphasizes the importance of logical modeling in creating efficient relational databases.

3. **Elmasri, R., & Navathe, S. B.** (2016). *Fundamentals of Database Systems* (7th ed.). Pearson.

This textbook is essential for understanding the theoretical foundations of database systems, offering in-depth explanations of data modeling, relational database design, and SQL.

4. **Teorey, T. J., Yang, S., & Fry, J. P.** (2011). *Database Modeling and Design: Logical Design* (4th ed.). Morgan Kaufmann.

Focused on the process of data modeling, this book explores the various types of logical models and provides practical insights for designing databases.

5. **McFadden, F. R., & Hoffer, J. A.** (2012). *Modern Database Management* (11th ed.). Pearson.

A textbook that offers a comprehensive treatment of database management, with particular attention to data modeling and design strategies.

6. **Ambler, S. W.** (2007). *Agile Database Techniques: Effective Strategies for the Agile Software Developer*. Wiley.

This book outlines best practices for applying agile methodologies to database design, including how to adapt data modeling techniques to agile development processes.

7. **Codd, E. F.** (1970). *A Relational Model of Data for Large Shared Data Banks*. *Communications of the ACM, 13*(6), 377–387.

A seminal paper that introduced the relational model of data, which serves as the foundation for most modern data modeling practices.

8. **Silberschatz, A., Korth, H. F., & Sudarshan, S.** (2011). *Database System Concepts* (6th ed.). McGraw-Hill.

   This book provides an in-depth understanding of database systems, including database design, relational databases, and the practical applications of data modeling.

9. **Finkelstein, L., & Davis, S.** (2008). *Data Modeling for the Business: A Handbook for Applying Patterns and Principles*. Wiley.

   This book offers practical advice on applying data modeling principles to business contexts, including guidelines for building robust, scalable data models.

10. **Martin, J.** (2004). *The Data Model Resource Book: A Library of Universal Data Models for All Enterprises* (Vol. 1). Wiley.

   A resource offering universal data models that can be applied across various business domains, with a focus on streamlining the design process for enterprise data systems.

11. **Inmon, W. H.** (2005). *Building the Data Warehouse* (4th ed.). Wiley.

   A foundational text on data warehousing that explores the integration of data models and techniques for structuring data across a range of business processes.

12. **Hainaut, J. L., & Roussel, J. P.** (2014). *Data Modeling: A Gentle Introduction*. Springer.

   This book provides a step-by-step guide to data modeling concepts, with a focus on providing easy-to-understand explanations for beginners.

13. **Gendron, P., & Bouchard, R.** (2013). *Entity Relationship Modeling for Business Systems Development*. Springer.

   A specialized text that delves into entity-relationship modeling, offering techniques for business analysts to apply these concepts to data-driven projects.

14. **Lenzerini, M.** (2002). *Data Integration: A Theoretical Perspective*. *Proceedings of the 21st ACM SIGMOD-SIGACT-SIGART Symposium on Principles of Database Systems (PODS)*, 233–246.

   This paper explores the complexities of integrating data from different sources and provides a theoretical framework for data modeling in multi-source systems.

15. **García-Molina, H., Ullman, J. D., & Widom, J.** (2009). *Database Systems: The Complete Book* (2nd ed.). Pearson.

Michael E. Kirshteyn, Ph.D

A comprehensive textbook on database systems, covering data modeling, transaction management, and query processing with a focus on relational database management systems (RDBMS).

These references are a mix of seminal works in the field of data modeling, practical textbooks, and applied methodologies in specific industries. They serve as foundational materials for readers wishing to deepen their understanding of data modeling concepts and practices.

Made in the USA
Las Vegas, NV
02 January 2025

15677997R00127